Belonge to

7-5-08

Students posed with books and a tennis racquet, symbolizing the importance of balancing life with friendship, study and other activities ~ Benzonia

Shared Moments:

A Journey Through Time

by the Benzie Area Historical Society

Signature Book Printing
Gaithersburg, Maryland

ISBN: 1-932433-91-0

Signature Book Printing
8041 Cessna Avenue
Gaithersburg, Maryland 20879

Acknowledgements:

We owe a tremendous debt of gratitude to the many people who made this book possible. Heartfelt thanks go to the following patrons who so generously sponsored the cost of underwriting this book:

Bill and Suzie Anderson
James Bayles
Maryellen Bieder
Florence Bixby
Walter and Diane Brutzer
James and Luanne Buzzell
Elizabeth Case
John and Rosemary Christenson
Robert and Janet Condon
Madonna Cussans
Gary and Ann Edwards
Fred and Carol Ehman
Richard and Sharon Eriksen
Bill and Karen Gilmore

Thor and Susan Goff
Patrick and Nancy Griffin
Walter Heath
Bob and Ginny Istnick
James and Eileen Kelly
Tim and Carole Krause
Peggy Martin
Ed and Jean McMullin
Melvin and Kay Noah
Paul and Barbara Odland
Bruce and Becky Ogilvie
The Palmer Family Fund
Bill and Joey Parris
Kip and Wendy Petherick

Jay Pettitt
Jane Purkis in memory of
    Ted Purkis
Ruth Reeve in memory of
    Joseph E. and
    Betty Washburn Reeve
Larry and Judith Ross
Jerry and Agnes Slater
Bruce and Jane Stowe
Helen Tanner
Dick and Bea Walters
Robert and Helen Wangard
Gerald and Frances Wyatt

Shared Moments: A Journey Through Time has been a huge undertaking for our committee and the Benzie Area Historical Society Board of Directors. Thousands of hours have been spent researching, locating, and selecting both historical photographs and the perfect quotes to go with them. We would like to thank the following collectors who so graciously donated the use of their photographs for this book:

Florence Bixby
The Allen Blacklock Collection courtesy of
    Deryl D. Holmes
Stacy Daniels
Jill Mendenhall and Bill Anderson
Bailey Family Collection
Carol Classens Beidler
Robert Beidler
Benzie Area Historical Museum
Benzie Shores District Library
Dan and Cindy Collier
Courtesy of the Crystal Lake Yacht Club
Empire Area Museum
Fran and Pat Forrester
Ann Reeves Franklin
Roger Griner
Don Harrison UpNorth Memories Collection
Joe and Kay Hommel

Al Hyams
Bob Kirshner
Jim Laarman
Almira Historical Society
The family of William and Agnes Olsen
Gretchen Peterson
Jane Purkis
Crystalaire Camp and Camp Lookout, Frankfort, MI
    Dave Reid and Katherine Houston, owners
Dana Robinson
Peter R. Sandman
Joyce Rodal Caveny
William H. Sharp
Ralph B. Rodal
The family of Augustus and Agnes Rogers
Courtesy of St. Ann Catholic Church
Charles Anderson and Carol Stack
Lawrence White

The photographs included in this book were obtained from independent collectors and from the comprehensive collection of the Benzie Area Historical Society, Benzie County, Michigan. The photographs have enabled our committee to put together a book which will fascinate people of all ages for generations to come. As the Benzie Historical Museum's purpose is to preserve history for posterity, our committee has created a book that not only serves that purpose, but leaves the reader with the feeling of having been there during the inception of Benzie County into the 1950s.

Photos have been brought to life for the viewer with the addition of wonderful quotes gathered from local authors and respected historians. In most cases the quotes have been presented exactly as written by the author without the correction of grammar, spelling, punctuation, etc. The written word of these authors, as printed, also helps to capture the time period in this book. For continuity purposes we have used ellipses (. . .) where we have eliminated words, phrases, lines, or paragraphs from within a quoted passage. A bibliography is included in the back of this book which lists authors and titles of the books quoted. We highly recommend them for your further enjoyment of the history of Benzie County, Michigan.

The included ten-minute DVD video, "Camp Days at Crystal Lake," presents summer life in the early 1900s, as described in recollections and photographs by members of the Wolfe Family. Special thanks to Larry White, producer and editor; Marian (Edwards) Doane, interviewer; Dean Edwards, graphic designer; and to Maryellen (Wolfe) Bieder, Helen (Wolfe) Dewey, Jean (Wolfe) Edwards, Ned Wolfe Edwards, Alice (Edwards) Hinkamp, Helen Hornbeck Tanner, Phoebe (Wolfe) Vance, Arthur Coffman Wolfe and James Snow Wolfe for providing photographs and historical information.

No book is complete without the expertise of competent proofreaders. Our sincere thanks to Florence Bixby for checking the book for historical correctness. Bixby is a well-known and respected historian of Benzie County. Thanks, too, to Carol Brouwer who helped with the laborious job of proofreading the text.

Our grateful thanks to Bill Anderson and members of the Benzie Area Historical Society Board of Directors for successfully obtaining patrons to help underwrite the cost of this book, which has made its publication possible.

Please forgive the committee for not including your favorite photograph, township, or location. Access to photographs dictated what we have used in this book. We worked diligently to cover all areas that have been a part of the evolution of Benzie County. However, it was impossible to do some communities justice due to the availability of photographs and the size of the book.

Our thanks to all of the members of the Board of Directors of the Benzie Area Historical Society, and to our families, for their support and patience during the intense period of planning, writing, working and worrying, which brought this book to fruition. It is a very difficult process to select thousands of photographs and post cards and then reduce them to the number used in this book. Our committee constantly joked that we needed to publish three volumes! We sincerely hope that you, your family, and friends, will enjoy our endeavor for years to come.

Shared Moments: A Journey Through Time
Book Committee:
Kay Hommel, Chairman
Carol Beidler
Kristine Clark
Jim Laarman
Kay Noah
William Pearson

Introduction

"Benzie County is beautiful no matter from where it is seen and from a height of a couple thousand feet it spreads out below in all its lovely entirety. There is the lush greenery of woods and orchards, the fifty lakes in much less than fifty minutes, the meandering Platte and Betsie Rivers, the winding road, the dazzling whiteness of bluffs and dunes, and always to the west, incomparable Lake Michigan rolling in from the distant horizon."

Case

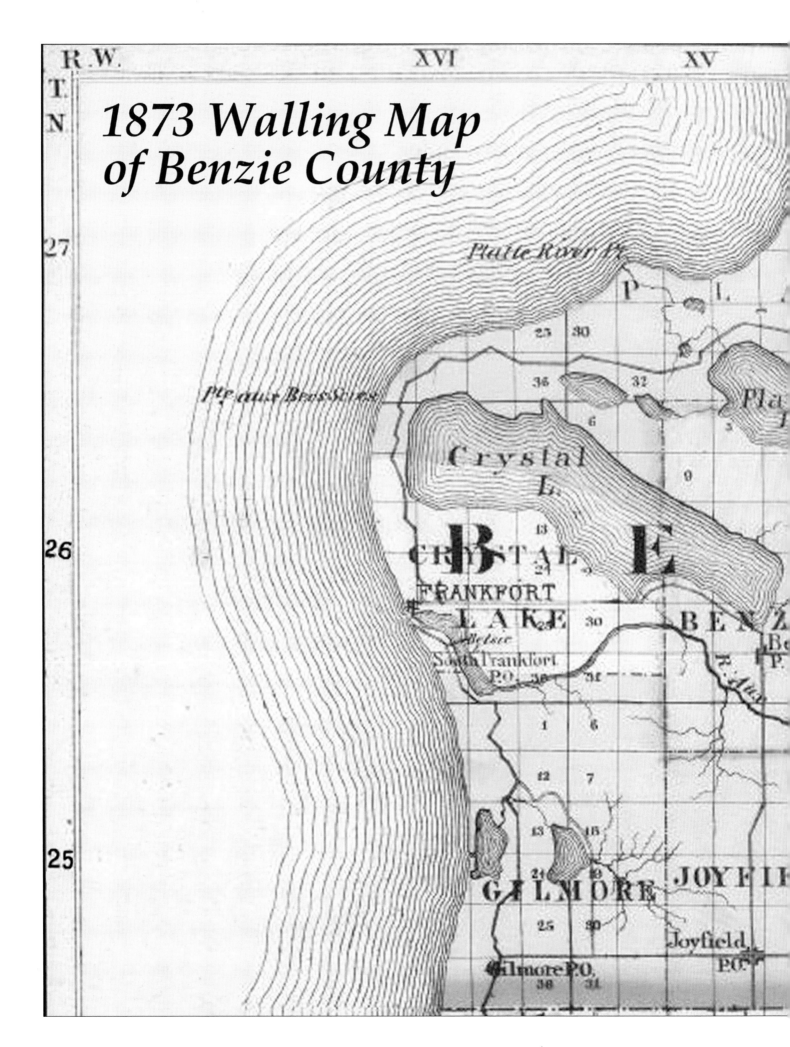

1873 Walling Map
of Benzie County

"Although relatively isolated from Michigan's tribal concentrations, Benzie County was a way station and seasonal campground for migrating Indians. The Ottawa migrated annually, ranging up and down Lake Michigan's eastern shoreline. They spent late fall and winter hunting and fishing along river banks in southern Michigan, and returned to their larger settlements in northern Michigan for spring planting."

Weeks
Grand Traverse Band of
Ottawa and Chippewa Indians

Haven From the Storm

The White Birch trees of northern Michigan had unique qualities that Native American Indians creatively put to use. Birch bark canoes were invented by the Ottawa Indians. They utilized nine layers of bark, stripped off in one piece, to form the skin of a canoe. The smaller pieces of bark were used like shingles on the walls of wigwams. This process afforded water-tight construction, and was also used on baskets. The flexible birch was fashioned into spears, bows, arrows, sleds, and snowshoes.

"Ettawageshik said there is a notion 'that pioneers came and out of nothing created civilization. But the very routes over which the pioneers came—the trails through the forests and the canoe portages between rivers—were the results of a people who had lived here thousands of years, who grew corn and squash and beans and traded and communicated with all parts of the country over this network of trails.' Early Indians established trails along the coastline to and from the shore where they fished and made camps."

Weeks
Grand Traverse Band of
Ottawa and Chippewa Indians

Father Marquette ~ Frankfort 1670 ~ died May 18, 1675

"The great Jesuit missionary, Father Marquette, was the first white man to set foot in what is now Benzie County."

John Howard

"….it was his Indian helpers who made his last moments easy, buried him on a sandy promontory, put up a cross to mark his grave, then slipped away northward to bear the news of his passing."

Catton

"As early as 1838 the government sent a surveyor, Alvin Burt, to survey the area [of Benzie County]. It is generally agreed by historians that it was about that time that the first non-Indian settler arrived . . . "

Bixby & Sandman

"The first white man to come to the Aux Bec Scies area was Joseph Oliver, a Pennsylvanian, who was here prior to 1847. Oliver's first wife was an Indian. He came as a guide for the first Government Surveyors. Oliver erected a small trapper's cabin near the outlet from Lake Aux Bec Scies to Lake Michigan and gained a living by hunting, fishing and trapping . . .

Joseph Oliver was a warm friend to the Indians and many of them traveled far out of their way to visit him. On one occasion an old Indian friend broke a small pane of glass from the window of the Oliver cabin by accident. The next morning, before daylight, the Indian disappeared only to return three days later with a glass for the window. He had walked to Traverse City and back to replace it."

Blacklock

"Had it not been for a fierce Lake Michigan gale, a ship and its captain, and his sighting of a safe harbor, the history of Frankfort's beginnings might have been quite different.

But there was a gale, and there was a ship, belonging to a wealthy ship owner in Buffalo, under the command of a Captain Snow. Finding his ship being buffeted ever nearer the shore, Captain Snow desperately sought an opening in the heavily timbered land and finding the mouth of the Aux Bec Scies River, he took a chance on navigating the shallow bar and at last found refuge from the storm in what is now Betsie Bay.

When the weather had cleared, Captain Snow made the return trip to Buffalo by way of Chicago and made his report concerning the wonderful natural harbor to the ship's owner George W. Tift.

This was in 1854 and it was not the beginning of Frankfort, but perhaps the beginning of the development of business here. George Tift bought land around the harbor.

Soon after that, about 1859, a group of men . . . bought all of Tift's land and organized the Frankfort Land Company calling this place Frankfort-On-The-Lake. George Frost was sent here to establish a settlement and open it up for business."

Bixby & Sandman

Finding a safe harbor was an open invitation for others to follow ~ c.1894

"Passengers and goods destined for Frankfort had to be lightered to land from the vessels standing some distance off shore. Four-footed live stock coming with the settlers were usually just heaved overboard to make their way to shore the best they could. No record is available as to whether domestic geese and ducks were lightered to shore, or were simply turned loose in the hopes they would follow in the wake of their quadraped friends."

Case

Schooner aground in Frankfort on Lake Michigan beach

"They had pumps aboard each schooner. Had pumps with handles, y'know. They'd get taking water and sometimes the crew would be pumpin' steady for twenty-four hours to keep the water out of'er 'til they could get in somewhere where they'd get taken care of. . . .All them big schooners I remember had a couple of pumps, one fore and one aft. It would throw a big stream of water."

Roy Oliver quote ~ *Overlease*

Nugent homestead ~ an early Frankfort family ~ summer of 1895

"The first living quarters usually put up by the early settlers were quite primitive affairs. William A. Joy describes the one that he built as an eight by ten pole shanty with a bark roof which he admits was a rather leaky affair, as during any kind of rain storm they had to pile all their goods in one corner and sit on them to keep them dry."

"The livestock on the farm consisted of one cow (it got sick and died), a calf (it wandered away and died), some chickens, and pigs. The Carvers gathered moss in the fall to seal the chinks between the logs in the chicken house but it didn't seem to do much good as the chickens would immediately proceed to peck it all out. Hawks were a menace to the chickens and although Mrs. Carver was somewhat fearful of Indians and black bears, she was very handy with an old shot gun and could bring down any soaring or diving predator birds with great accuracy."

Case

Axel Frederickson homestead ~ one of the first open wells (wooden box to right) ~ Crystal Lake Township ~ 1897

" . . . in all portions of the area carved out of the old Northwest Territory, a homesteader had to stay on his land in order to establish his claim to it. The nameless historian tells of one settler who was digging a well on his property and was down about 40 ft. with it when it showed signs of caving in. His wife arrived at the scene just at the critical time and seeing the situation shouted to her husband forty feet below 'Faith and be jabbers, if it should come down on ye, you'd hold your homestead for sure.'"

Case

Developing our Resources

Notch cut to fell this huge pine tree was large enough to hold a man ~ the scale of lumbering was immense

"By the 1870s, lumbering became the most important industry in Benzie County and the village and harbor, with its location on the big lake, was a beehive of activity."

Bixby & Sandman

Lumbering Days

"In the early days . . . the bunk shanty originally was simply a rectangular building of chinked logs, with no floor but the packed earth. Bunks were ranged along the wall, and the heat came from an open fire in a shallow pit in the middle of the room. There was no chimney, overhead there was a slot in the roof, and most of the smoke went out there. Windows there were none, and the bunk shanty was as smoky, ill-ventilated and generally smelly as any living quarters man has ever used. . . . . the lumberjack never saw his camp in daylight except on Sundays—he went off into the forest before sunrise and he came back after dusk, and he knew his homeplace only as a warm spot in the cold darkness, where he ate and slept and on Sunday boiled his socks and long johns and waged ineffective war on bedbugs that infested the bunkhouse. . . . If you lived through a winter in the steamy, malodorous dimness of a lumber camp shanty, you belonged, you were a shanty boy, then and thereafter."

Catton

Cutting bark to be used for tanning leather

"Logs! Logs! Logs! — nothing but logs! Bark is being shipped in large quantities and the loads are very big." *February 15, 1900*

Benzie Banner

"The man who worked in the woods was caught in a bind. The lumber camp did not offer a decent annual income. Wage rates varied . . . but the logger generally got twenty-five or thirty dollars a month and his work year was only six months long."

"Though the housing improved, the life remained hard. The men were out in the woods as soon as the sun came up – the get'em up cry in the bunk shanty was a chanted 'Daylight in the Swamp'—and the foreman went about indicating the trees that were to be felled."

Catton

Big wheels were used to move logs

"I mostly done skidding in camp. I'd haul lots down, and I'd do a big wheel some, too, but not very much. That was for summer loggin', that's the only way they could get logs in the summer with big wheels or trucks." *Bob Bailey* quote

"Well, in my time, the typical lumberjack was the guy that comes from the laboring class of people. He was un-educated and he is out-moded, now we might say, by the march of progress."

Overlease

Using the snow to advantage and transporting the logs on sleighs with runners ~ Crystal Lake Township

"The prize guys, the top guys in the lumber camp was a top loader, sky hooker, they called him. He was the guy that after the bunk was full of logs, he got up on and built this load. The guy that could build a load, it took skill because you had to keep the sides straight, you see . . . you had to get a big load, you had to keep those sides straight, and that was the skill it took and the top loader, he got bigger money than anyone else."

Overlease

Hauling 5,782 board feet of logs through the icy streets of Honor

"In the winter they'd come down into town there, and they had these sprinklers that was made like a big box. There were sprinkle booms right close. They'd walk along behind because that water had to come just a certain way. That would freeze to make a good, I believe you'd call it a proper footing, for the sleighs when they came down. The most beautiful teams of horses bringin' all those logs in. There weren't a kid in town that didn't ride on those logs if they got a chance."

Overlease

"It was up to the teamster to drive the sleigh along the glare ice of a roadway two or three miles to the banking grounds, an open place on the bank of the nearest river where the logs were stacked in enormous piles that would be tumbled into the water when spring came."

Catton

Rivermen moving piled logs from the banking grounds into the river after the spring thaw ~ c. 1892

"In one way or another the winter's cut of logs was finally stacked up along a river, and when spring came, the camp's work was over. . . . as the lumber camps paid off their men and closed, the business of transporting the logs to the mills got under way. Originally everything went by water . . . and now it was the river man who was all important."

Catton

Rivermen running a river of logs ~ Betsie River

"Michigan's great white pine era was just getting underway, and grandfather waded right into the middle of the operation. His specialty was working the river drives – cold, wet, dangerous work."

Barnard

"A log drive that contained one and one half million board feet of lumber, a winter's cut for an average camp, would fill a major river, bank to bank, for two miles."

Catton

Cutting up logs on site with a large transportable power saw

Using a steam driven machine to lift logs onto a flatbed railroad car ~ c.1910

Loaded flatbed railroad cars quickly transported logs to the mills

Mill fires were common; fast but limited help came from water barrels placed on the roof ~ Platte Edgewater Mill ~ c.1880-1900

"In operating sawmills . . . there had to be a crew for each mill. The sawmills crew took up where the woodsmen and lumber jacks left off in the job of converting the trees of the forests into lumber for the market. And while the men of the mill crew were a hardy and hard working breed, they were usually a little different type of men than the lumber jacks.

The mill men were more apt to be men of families living in their homes in the vicinity of the mill and within walking distance of the mill although it might have been a mile or two or three away. Each morning they would set out toting their tin dinner pails which were topped by a coffee compartment . . . and plod through snow usually before the light of day."

Case

Up-scale mill housing ~ c.1910

"Normally the homes of a mill town were thrown together by the lumberjacks and were made of rough boards covered with tarpaper, and so was the mill. After all, they were only to be used for two or three years, five at the most."

Chapman

Francis Bailey, son of Solomen Bailey, owner of Solomen Bailey and Sons mill

Solomen Bailey & Sons Mill ~ an Indian owned and operated logging company with all Indian crew during Cold Creek Flood ~ c.1910

"Indians frequently dealt in tan bark and would load their canoes with about half a cord of bark, when the canoe rail would be barely three inches above the water. They then stood up in the canoes and threw the wood and bark six or eight feet up into the schooners."

Bixby & Sandman

Bull Donkey Engine ~ Elberta sawmill

Lumber stacks ~ 3 stories high!

"By the early 1880s, or perhaps a bit earlier, this industry found itself limited by nothing whatever except two things that were utterly beyond its control—the appetite of the market, and the supply of its raw material. The appetite of the market . . . seemed to be unlimited; the source of supply unfortunately was not."

Catton

The lumbermen cut and moved on ~ c. 1905

"The lusty lumberjacks left behind . . . cut-over areas where only stumps and rotting tops and underbrush remained . . . .

Stadtfeld

Removing the "stumps" was not a simple task ~ c.1910

"When lumber was depleted, much of the area returned to farming."

Bixby & Sandman

Little chicks

"The chicken's care was 'woman's work.'. . . Women, usually more practical than men, were glad to have the chickens for their fresh eggs and fresh meat, and for pin money, and if that meant they had to take care of them, so be it. . . . Much of our youth was devoted to a steady initiation process, taking a little more responsibility and a little more work as we grew larger, stronger, more skillful, until the transition to full responsibility seemed so natural it was hardly noticed. There were plenty of chores, and we grew into them one by one."

Stadtfeld

Threshing time ~ a family affair

Bringing in the hay ~ everyone contributed

"Horses had to be bought; few men raised colts. A team would be bought for 40 acres, but a farmer with 80 needed at least three horses and a quarter section (160 acres) required five or six. Two horses drew a single-moldboard, 10-inch walking plow, and could cover an acre a day. A slightly larger riding plow took three horses. . . .Hay was mowed by a machine, then bunched with a dump rake. Handwork was required to make those bunches into round piles, the size of a big fork load. The piles were tossed onto a wagon, the load divided into layers by rope and slat slings. The load was then hauled to the barn where the horses were unhitched and let out singly beside the wagon and hitched again to the track at the top of the barn and down to hooks that raised the sling loads of hay so they could be shunted into the mows and dumped."

Stadtfeld

Three Horse Plow Team ~ ready for work ~ c.1910

"Horses were a very important factor in the development of this area and a vital necessity to business, industry and agriculture."

"Will Schafer, the livery owner, had a sick horse. The horse was down and seemed ready to die. Mr. Schafer said he would sell him for 10 cents. Al McConnell, one of the crowd gathered at the event took him up and gave him the dime. McConnell then went to the Collins Drug Store, two doors away, and had the druggist mix him up a prescription that would have moved a 'Rock.' Al got this down the horse and within the hour had him on his feet. The next day he plowed with him and several weeks later sold him back to Schafer for $25.00. True story. I was there."

Blacklock

Best Friends

"Gilmore, like Benzonia, had its bear scares, but the actual appearance of these ursine creatures were scarce. The only authenticated appearance was attested to by a woman who set out one afternoon to round up her cows. Before coming upon the cows, she came upon a big black bear, frightening them both and each taking off in different directions. The bear was later traced and shot down and the history does not record whether the woman ever found her cows or not." *(According to this photo, she found at least one!)*

Case

Oxen cart hauling barrels of water to the workers ~ Benzie/Leelanau County Line ~ c.1907

Everyone wore straw hats picking raspberries ~ Keeler Raspberry Farm

While many workers were local, successful agriculture also depended upon the skills of migrant workers. They arrived when needed most, worked hard, and then moved on when the crops were harvested. While residing in the community, they attended our churches, shopped in our stores, and contributed to the local economy.

Cherry Orchard with a profitable new angle

"And now the fruit growers have come up with a profitable new angle; convincing vacationers how much fun it is to pick their own fruit to take home."

Barnard

Picking peaches had its ups and downs

" . . . for a long period of years peaches became perhaps the most stable crop that came from the ground where timber had been removed."

Howard

"There is nothing degrading about hand labor; someone has to do it. And a certain amount is good for the constitution. But I strongly suspect that if we nostalgia buffs were to admit the truth, we would have jumped at the chance to have found an easier way to draw our wages."

Barnard

Wide brimmed hats protected pickers from the sun while harvesting the potato crop ~ Frankfort

"Next to where the railroad once crossed through the village . . . stood the potato warehouse. . . . After the hardwood in the area was exhausted, the farmers grew potatoes and sold them to the owner of the warehouse. There was a basement under the entire building. A rope bucket elevator was originally the only way to get to and from the basement. Not only were the potatoes carried down in this contraption, but the men had to ride in this also. George Habbler got hung upside down on this once, and they just left him to get out by himself."

Brosier

On the way to market ~ c.1910

Trapp celery fields ~ Beulah

Trapp Greenhouse and Celery Farms ~ Beulah c.1930

"The young plants were brought to us from the greenhouse in wooden flats. . . . When the plants got well established, we were put to weeding them; this was done on dry fields and all on hands and knees. After a few hours, those rows seemed to have no end. . . . My wage starting out was ten cents an hour, by my fourth year I had worked up to seventeen. . . . However, goods were priced accordingly: a large slab of pie or hamburger cost a dime, ice cream cone, pop or candy bar a nickel. . . . . During those four years Walt and I bought most of our own school clothes, furnished our own spending money, and bought two cars, a 1928 Model-A Ford for $25.00 and a 1934 V-8 Ford from Ernie Stiles for $45.00."

" . . . Trapp's broke some new ground in the Platte River Swamp area for raising onions. . . . When the men were clearing the ground, they found, and killed, quite a number of Massaeauga rattlesnakes. It is the only place in our part of northern Michigan I ever heard of having these snakes. We boys were pretty leery of working over there, but no one ever got struck by one."

Barnard

Taking produce to market ~ c.1940

"The crops (celery and head lettuce) were harvested by the men using butcher type knives, then trucked to the wash house on Cold Creek. The produce was washed and packed in boxes mostly by women and girls, then stored in the refrigerated building. The produce was delivered to area stores and some out-of-state locations."

Barnard

Memories ~ after World War II farming in Benzie County almost died out ~ only the fruit growers flourished

"The barns are empty, and the grass grows in the barnyard fence rows. The places look a little shaggy, as though something that belongs there has vanished."

"Like . . . other farm boys in those years, I left not in anger, not in retreat, but in search of new promise. My parents and theirs could not know that we could never really go away, never push from our lives those rich years on the farm. . . . We did not deceive our parents or our pasts; the times did, and we were captives of the times, as captive as our parents were. We saw new sounds and heard new lures, sought new places and found new lives. But we never really left, and the soil is still in our souls."

Stadtfeld

Fishing tug "Comet" ~ Olsen Fisheries ~ Frankfort Harbor

Some people firmly believe that commercial fishing was the first industry in Benzie County ~ fishermen unloading the nets ~ c.1940s

"In the 20s and 30s there were 22 fishing tugs operating from the Frankfort harbor with crews of at least three men each. This provided a living for more than 60 families. . . . By 1937 over 10,000 pounds of fish per day were trucked to Thompsonville and shipped from there [overnight] by rail to markets in the cities."

Bixby & Sandman

Fishing tug coming in with the day's catch at Anderson Fisheries ~ c.1900

"During the years of 1900 until the 1920s, most of the fish tugs were of steam power and used coal in their boilers. Each fish tug had a railroad track to their coal shed. . . . Dick Strauble usually unloaded the coal by the shovel. He would unload a car in the day, from daylight to dark for 25 cents per ton. He would make $13.75 for the day's work. After the car was unloaded, he would head for Carl Muelhman's for a few drinks . . . ."

Anderson

Jean-R's deck hands lifting the nets ~ c.1940

"During the summer months, we would leave the dock at 4 a.m. . . . We would lift 24 boxes of nets and also set back 24 boxes of nets. One box of nets was about 2,000 ft. We usually arrived back in Frankfort 8:30 – 10:30 at night. We would pack the fish in ice, 100 lbs. to the box."

Anderson

Nets required drying and constant repair

"There were many ways of fishing, but the two most commonly used methods for commercial fishing were with either the gill net or the pound net. Which net you would use depended on the location you were going to set your nets and what fish you were trying to catch."

Anderson

Great Lakes Sturgeon ~ 1940s

"The commercial fishermen pulled in their nets daily and sometimes there were surprises. I remember my uncle finding a Great Lakes sturgeon in the net (which was illegal to keep). Our extended family enjoyed it after it was broiled over an open fire. I still remember how good it tasted!"

Clark

Checking nets for damage ~ 1940s

"The fishing business began to decline during the 1940s due to many factors. Some to over-fishing, but the greatest decline in the trout fishing was due to some of the predators that ate the eggs from the spawning beds, such as fish ducks."

Anderson

"The noisy gulls had a celebration of their own, hovering about the
fortunate fishermen as they cleaned their catches." ~ 1948
The Detroit News

Look what I caught! ~ a large Mackinaw Trout (with lamprey eel wound)

"Then in 1943, we begin to get many lamprey eels attached to the lake trout. . . . In four years, it didn't pay us to fish for them anymore. We then began to fish chubs, so the price went down to 8 – 10 cents per pound. We were soon forced to suspend our fishing operation and lay up the 'Evelyn S.' (fishing tug) and pay off our crew of six men."

"We sold the 'Evelyn S.' in 1952. . . . When I started the engine to take her to her new home in Muskegon, it was a very sad day for me. Yes, I shed a tear and watched her head south for Muskegon. It was losing a dear old friend."

Anderson

"The fishing began to decline with the start of World War II and by the early 1960s the last of the fishing operations closed."

Bixby & Sandman

Celebrating! First Passenger Train in Benzie County ~ the Frankfort & South Eastern (later the Ann Arbor Railroad) ~ July 4, 1889

Michigan Governor "James M. Ashley had a dream, a vision of building a railroad from Toledo, Ohio in a northwesterly direction up through the state of Michigan to Lake Michigan to Wisconsin ports. His vision became a plan and the plan a reality of the greatest import to the economic well-being of Elberta and the surrounding area, as Elberta became the northern terminus of Ashley's Railroad and the Marine Terminal for his Carferry Operation."

Blacklock

Beulah Train Depot

"This is how it was in the old days. A family that wanted to go from here to there went by railroad train because there was no other way to do it. If the distance was short, ten or a dozen miles only, you might hire a rig at the livery stable and let the horses do the work, and if you lived on deep water you might go all or part of the way by steamboat, but as a general thing to make a trip meant to take a ride on the cars."

"We always began by going to the railroad station at Beulah. . . . The trip to Beulah was unexciting – no driver in his senses drove down that hill at anything but a plodding walk – but once we reached the depot the atmosphere changed and we began to understand that we were really going somewhere."

Catton

"Ready to go" on the Morning Train

"Then at last, just as the tension was almost more than we could take, we could hear the train as it rounded Outlet Point and came along the lake shore, the clear notes of its whistle sounding across the water, and finally it would drift around the last curve and swing up to the platform, smoking and hissing and clanking, with the locomotive putting on its characteristic act of looking and sounding like something alive. A few passengers would get off, and the conductor would call a long-drawn 'all ab-o-o-a-r-d!' and we would scramble up the steps . . . ."

Catton

Waiting for the passengers at Empire Junction ~ Platte Township

"It was even better when we took the night train because to ride in a sleeping car was to touch the summit of human experience. . . . Getting undressed in the berth of an old-style twelve-section sleeping car meant that you almost had to be a contortionist. Getting your pants off, for instance, required you to lie on your back, arch yourself until you were supported by your heels and your shoulders, and start fumbling."

Catton

The "Ping Pong" train was strictly a summer attraction

"Around 1910, the Ann Arbor operated what they called the 'Ping Pong' passenger train. It traveled from Frankfort to Thompsonville every two hours in the summer time. In the winter it made the trip once a day."

Gibbs

"The 'Ping Pong' would run from Frankfort to Beulah head first with the locomotive ahead of the coach. There being no 'Y' or turn table at [the other end], it must make the return trip in reverse all the way. The 'Ping Pong,' bless its good old iron heart, provided to many a Benzie County child his first and perhaps to some, his only experience of ever having ridden on a passenger train."

Case

Ann Arbor & Pere Marquette section crews ~ Thompsonville Depot 1903

"A really important, and most familiar, crew were the section men. They had to do everything no one else would, or could do, besides their own work on the tracks. They spread the track ballast, cinders, gravel, and later crushed stone. Laid the ties and tamped them in and spiked the rails to them. They also had to keep the track on grade. They kept the switches oiled and repaired and cleaned out the ice and snow in the winter and spread sand or cinders on the switch leads when slippery with ice."

Blacklock

"All Aboard" ~ Thompsonville Depot where the Pere Marquette and Ann Arbor Railroads crossed the "Diamond" ~ 1919

"Several railroads were being built in 1889. The Toledo, Ann Arbor & North Michigan Railroad was completed from Toledo, Ohio, to the Manistee County town of Copemish, three miles southeast of Thompsonville. In the same year, the Frankfort & Southeastern Railroad was completed from Copemish through Thompsonville to the Lake Michigan port of Frankfort, a distance of 24 miles. About this same time, the Chicago & West Michigan Railroad was completed through Thompsonville from Chicago to Petoskey.

Both railroads staged a race to see who would get to Thompsonville first, as the loser would have to lay the 'diamond' and have to maintain it in the cross tracks. The Chicago & West Michigan Railroad won the race, so the Toledo, Ann Arbor and North Michigan laid the 'diamond.'. . . In 1892, the Frankfort & Southeastern Railroad was sold to the Toledo, Ann Arbor & North Michigan Railroad and in 1893, the entire line went bankrupt. It was thereafter operated as the Ann Arbor Railroad. That's why we called it the intersection of the Pere Marquette and Ann Arbor!"

Gibbs

Teamsters waiting to unload the boxcars ~ South Frankfort (Elberta)

"The farmers made good use of the railroad, and hay and grain was delivered along the route in addition to groceries and supplies from the company store. Passengers were welcome to a free ride at their own risk."

Blacklock

Hard work on the tracks calls for a break! ~ Nesson City Depot, and Manistee & North Eastern Section Crew ~ c.1890s

*Train wreck on Bay Point, Crystal Lake Township (later
called Railroad Point) ~ near Crystal Lake outlet ~ c.1911*

Horrible aftermath of a train wreck! ~ Ann Arbor No. 185 at Pomona ~ July 4, 1929

"The exact location of that train wreck was half a mile east of Pomona on the steep grades which were hard for the old steam engines to pull up a hundred-car train. They would leave half a train and half the cars at Harlan and come back from Mesick and get the second half because it's all down-grade from Mesick to Copemish.

On the night of the big wreck, heavy rains washed out about 100 feet of the rail bed. Early in the night . . . the southbound freight trains came over the grade that was still in good condition. They stopped at the Harrietta by-pass and the engineers from both the southbound and northbound talked to each other. Northbound #185 was behind schedule, and as the Pomona area coming up was all downgrade, the engineer wanted to make up extra time. . . . In the meantime, the rains washed out 300 feet of the railroad grade. So when the steam engine and train cars went over the washed out grade, the train rolled on its side and slid for some distance before coming to a stop. The engineer and the fireman were killed and twenty railcars derailed. . . . Crushed and splintered cars were piled up four deep behind the engine. . . . The wreck was scattered all over the site."

Griner

Waiting for the U.S. Mail ~ Manistee & North Eastern Depot ~ Lake Ann

"The railroad that passed through the village of Lake Ann was the Manistee & North Eastern. The train left Traverse City in the morning and went to Manistee and returned in the afternoon. The mail was sorted on the train. . . . The sorter on the train was fast. He would kick the mailbag out at any village on the route, and the station manager at each place would throw the bag of mail on at the same time. . . ."

Brosier

End of the line ~ Ann Arbor Railroad Engine #2183 on the turntable ~ Elberta

Ann Arbor Railroad Engine off the turn table

"When the steam engines came in from their run on the road or their shift in the yard, they had to be serviced. The hostler took them to the water spout, filled the tank with water, stopped at the sand house, and filled the sand box, then moved to the cinder pit where the fire was shook out. Then, across the turntable, with the steam that was left and to the roundhouse stall, where the machinist and the boiler-maker and their helpers did the necessary work to prepare them for another run."

Blacklock

The old and the new ~ early entrance to the Frankfort Harbor

"Sunday, November 27, 1892, marked an epoch not only in the history of Kewaunee [Wisconsin], but in that of the whole country and is the most notable event of the generation in the annals of navigation. On that day, a train of loaded cars was successfully transferred bodily sixty miles across an open and stormy body of water. . . . After much straining of eye-sight and many slighting remarks by the incredulous, smoke was discerned in the direction of Frankfort and within an hour the monster leviathan car-ferry steamer Ann Arbor No.1, without a flag flying or a whistle blowing, and without as much commotion as is made by a tug, steamed majestically into the harbor and backed into the slip prepared for her, as if the business had been an every day occurrence for her for years. . . ."

Frederickson

Carferry No. 2 in Betsie Bay Harbor prior to the construction of the Hotel Frontenac ~ 1898

"It will probably surprise as well as interest the resorter unversed in Frankfort's early history to learn that the first channel from Betsey Lake into Lake Michigan was not where the deep channel now is and where the long piers are projected. That site was originally but a sand hill near the shore . . . and it was only 3-4 ft. deep. Until a dredge, some years later than the advent of the first white settlers, approached from the outside and dredged its way through, this meager channel was navigable only for rowboats and light-draft cargos of lumber towed in for building purposes."

Howard

Carferry No. 1 ~ the first carferry on Lake Michigan

"One of the outstanding features of the Ann Arbor No.1 was that she was the first triple screw boat ever used in this country. . . . The bow was designed to run up on the ice and break it with the weight of the vessel. . . . She was built to carry 24 cars (which were smaller then), and when she first came out, she made about 14 miles per hour. . . . It cost about $260,000 to build her."

Frederickson

"About 9 a.m., forty minutes after Boat 4's departure, the soft falling snow had changed into a howling blizzard and the temperature dropped rapidly. The storm broke in all its fury . . .

At 4:50 a.m. out of that howling blizzard came the dreaded signal which I had feared all night might be sent. 'SOS SOS WFK WFK. . . . returning to the East Shore in a sinking condition. Have lost two cars overboard. Deck covered with foot of ice and stanchions on car deck have buckled allowing deck to fall a foot I hope . . . we can make it.'

Yet again at 6:45 a.m., 'SOS SOS WDO hit south pier broadside, pounding badly and breaking up.'

By 9:30 or 10 a.m. it had cleared sufficiently that Boat 4's predicament could be seen. Some of the Coast Guards volunteered to go out to Boat 4 on the South Pier to deliver the orders . . . That . . . the crew must be removed. As I recall it, two Coast Guards tied themselves together with thirty or forty feet of line and made their way slowly out to Boat 4 by the aid of ice spurs on their shoes and ice picks to keep them from sliding off the pier which was rounded over with slippery ice. The crew came ashore in two groups and everyone breathed a sigh of relief when the last of the crew had reached safety because here was a catastrophe that might have ended much differently and saddened many homes in (the area). . . ."

Blacklock

Carferry No. 4 broke up after hitting Frankfort's South Pier broadside

Crew surveying the damaged interior of the ship

Divers on the wreck of Carferry No. 4

"Boat 4 lay on the bottom, against the Elberta Pier until spring, when the Reed Wrecking Co. . . raised her . . . . Necessary repairs were made. . . . She was returned to service October 7, 1923, and received a royal salute by all the whistles the two villages could muster."

Blacklock

Breaking up the ice while leaving the harbor

"The A.A. No. 5 was built as an icebreaker, for heavy winter ice had often held up the other boats in the fleet. Often forced to break ice more than 2 ft. thick, she was known to have made her way through more than 36" of solid blue ice, and in 20 ft. of water to have pushed through fields of ice that extended to the bottom. Not only did she lead the way, making channels for the other ships of the line to follow, but she was also the fastest ship. . . ."

Frederickson

Stoking the boilers ~ a very hot job!

Boxcars loaded and braced inside carferry ~ a necessary safety precaution

Life boat drill turned to photo op!

Carferry Slip ~ Ann Arbor Docks ~ South Frankfort (Elberta)

Carferry loading boxcars ~ c.1915

"In 1928 the Ann Arbor had six car-ferry steamers and made 4,300 trips across the lake and carried nearly 100,000 freight cars."

Blacklock

"Over the years the harbor has played an important role in the life of Frankfort and Elberta [South Frankfort]. The earliest improvements deepened the channel and piers were constructed. Later improvements were made with the south breakwater being completed in 1931. In 1932 the north breakwater was finished and the lighthouse was remodeled. Thus Frankfort Harbor became a safe harbor for a variety of water craft."

Bixby & Sandman

Leaving town ~ Ann Arbor Carferry No. 7

"Boat #7 cost about one million dollars. Besides the 12 modern, commodious staterooms, she has a large spacious cabin, observation and smoking room, also a beautiful dining room finished in natural grained light oak seating 35 people with large windows along the outboard side which affords a pleasant view of all passing scenery. . . . While in the ship yards for repairing a bent rudder on August 25, 1925, the entire crew knocked off work to attend the Manitowoc County Fair. They all came back sober."

Frederickson

. . . and then there is the story about Ole:

"Ole Olsen worked as a wheelsman on the Ann Arbor No. 7 . . . Ole Glarum was First Mate. One day he fired Ole Olsen. Ole Glarum went home while the boat was unloading and then loading. Later, when they got out on the lake, Glarum went on his watch in the pilot house and Ole Mick Olsen was at the wheel, steering the boat. Glarum said to him, 'I fired you.' Ole said, 'Yes, I know, but I like it here. I'll tell you when I want to quit.' Ole was a very witty, intelligent person."

Anderson

Construction of the Royal Frontenac Hotel ~ Frankfort 1901

"Now the Royal Frontenac was the pride of Frankfort town. It had been built in 1901 by the Ann Arbor Railroad Company, on the waterfront facing Lake Michigan as a summer hotel of magnificent proportions. Five hundred feet long it was. Three stories high and hundreds of rooms. Colonaded verandas swept around both sides and one end of the upper two floors. A wide concrete sidewalk completely encircled it."

Glazer

Halcyon days were about to end ~ 1912

"A good fire will always attract everyone within walking, running, or riding distance and on this night, although the hour was late and the weather cold, Frankfort turned out almost to the last man, woman, and child. The Eagle's Hall was emptied of its dancers without benefit of 'Good Night Ladies,' bed clothes were flung aside and whatever street clothes could be snatched up were hastily donned, cards were scattered, and card tables upset without the pot being counted, books and newspapers were thrown to the floor, ear phones of a few primitive radio sets were quickly removed from listening ears, and from all points of the town running, pounding feet made the cold, crusty snow crack as they bore their owners to the scene of the devastation." *The Hotel Frontenac burned to the ground on that cold January night in 1912.*

Case

Hotel fires were common and drew a crowd ~ Hotel Yeazel ~ Frankfort c.1920

All that was left

Hotel Diamond ~ Thompsonville ~ c.1911

"This hotel was a very popular hostelry during the days when activity at Thompsonville was at its height. It was a favorite stopping place for persons making connections for both the Ann Arbor and Pere Marquette trains, it being situated less than a block from junction of the two roads."

Case

Having a wonderful time! ~ a camping party at the Ottawa Resort ~ Crystal Lake 1895

"So permanent buildings of moderate cost began to spring up here and there. . . . Finally a little group of these temporary abodes took on the dignified name of a 'resort.'"

Howard

Quaint comfort at Chimney Corners Resort ~ Crystal Lake ~ 1912

Watervale Resort ~ after the lumbering days were over ~ Blaine Township ~ 1907

Watervale on the South Shore of Lower Herring Lake was, at one time, a busy village with a saw mill, store, and post office. After the lumber activity ceased, it was virtually abandoned.

For a while, Watervale was used as a private hunting camp. In 1918, it became a popular family-owned resort and remains so today.

Keeping the children busy with activities ~ in front of old post office ~ Watervale Resort

Enjoying the beautiful view of Crystal Lake on the veranda of the Northway Hotel ~ Beulah ~ c.1948

Getting up nerve for the "high dive" ~ Northway Hotel ~ Beulah c.1948

"One of the most famous resort hotels in Beulah was the Northway Hotel located on Crystal Lake in back of the Beulah Drug Store. It was a large white wood-framed structure with shutters, potted plants, and wicker furniture adorning the inside and outside of the building. The hotel served as a lovely summer hotel where college girls, dressed in black uniforms and white aprons, served dinners to guests as they dined in the large, bright dining room overlooking Crystal Lake."

Sproul

Ready to serve ~ the wait staff at the Koch Hotel ~ Frankfort

"The Koch Hotel, located on Leelanau Avenue, was known as a small, exclusive hotel that served splendid meals. Known for their Hungarian Goulash and Yankee Pot Roast, people used to stand in line to get in."

Sproul

Van Winkle Hotel on Crystal Lake ~ near the northern end of the Ann Arbor Railroad line ~ 1890—1895

Louis VanWinkle built this hotel at the urging of the Ann Arbor Railroad. He operated it about 1890 to 1895, but lost it in the panic of 1895. It later burned.

The Windemere Hotel ~ Beulah

"In that not too distant past, summer hotels were a going and very popular institution in the resort areas of the country. In Benzie County, several of them thrived. One such hotel was the Windemere. . . .

The Windemere was built in 1903. . . .Room and board per week, per guest, was $27.50. . . . It contributed considerably to the local economy. Many a high school girl and several high school boys found their summer employment there. Local grocery stores and fresh produce growers made daily deliveries of supplies. Its dock was a port of call in the days when passenger boats were making daily scheduled trips around the lake."

Glazer

Pitching tents and camping out has always been a great way to enjoy the outdoors

From tents to trailers ~ Trailer Park on Crystal Lake ~ Beulah ~ 1949

"The charms of Crystal Lake could not be reserved for the enjoyment of the local resident and the chance visitor. The story of its attractions was carried afar . . . Its rustic marges began to be the scene of occasional camping parties, desultory at first, but growing in favor. Then for a few tired townspeople and their more intimate friends . . . the love of 'camping out' developed into habit. . . ."

Howard

Awesome Dreams

"The Camp" ~ Settling in on Crystal Lake ~ 1906

"On October 6, 1904, my great-grandparents, Augustus J. and Jane P. Rogers, bought 69.6 acres along the north shore of Crystal Lake for $550. In the summer of 1905, they contracted to build a 16x24 foot tent platform and a building for a kitchen on the bluff. The construction and the tent together cost $60. Later, around 1911, when their son was building his home in the near-by orchard, a larger building with 2 bedrooms made of burlap walls and a living space with a stone fireplace was added to replace the tent. Back then 'the camp' had shuttered window openings with no glass and no screens. The original buildings are still used today with many modern conveniences added."

Agnes Slater

Three generations ~ the passage of time brought improvements in housing

"In those days of early settlement, it was a quiet land. The muscles of men and beast cleared the land and reaped the harvests, and a man could hear himself, his neighbor, and quite literally his God, as he worked. . . . The crows stood their ground and cawed a protest against every invasion of their sanctuary. Their calls were among the loudest sounds."

Stadtfeld

The wonderful aroma of freshly baked bread drifted from kitchens such as this ~ Benzonia

Washing her hair on the porch on a warm, sunny day

Washday was a lot more difficult then ~ but look at that lovely smile!!

Preparing dinner ~ overkill on that chicken!

A gracious early Victorian home ~ Frankfort

"The people are enterprising, and social advantages are excellent."

The Traverse Region

Elegant architecture and craftsmanship evolved ~ George Spence home built in 1898 ~ Benzonia

George Spence was the village blacksmith with a shop on Main Street, Benzonia.

First Congregational Church ~ Frankfort

"In 1867, Mr. and Mrs. Jacob Voorheis organized a Bible class and Sunday School and were instrumental in getting clergymen to come and hold services at their home. In 1868, the Congregational Church was organized, and in 1871 the sum of $5,000 was raised to build the church edifice, which with a few improvements is still located at the corner of Fifth and Forest Avenue."

Seabury

Scandinavian Church ~ Frankfort

"The first Lutheran service in Frankfort was held on October 1, 1882. The actual organization of the congregation took place on (October 15, 1882) and members continued to hold services in their homes and public buildings as places of worship.

In 1885, the congregation began to construct a church building. . . .The building site was donated by the local real estate and lumbering firm of Day and Butler. One dollar was given to legalize the transaction.

On April 8, 1886, the constitution of the 'Skandinaviske Evangeliske Lutherske Menighed' in Frankfort was adopted."

Bixby & Sandman

Congregational Church ~ Benzonia ~ the present site of the Benzie Area Historical Museum

Miss Lou's Sunday School Class

"Early in the 1850s, Congregationalists came to this area to found the community of Benzonia and a Christian college. In 1860, the Reverend Charles E. Bailey, prime figure behind the organization of the community and college, helped organize the area's first church with eighteen members. Erected in 1884/87, this Gothic Revival style building served the congregation until 1968. In 1969, the building became the Benzie Area Historical Museum."

Michigan History Division
Department of State

Worship services at the Congregational Church ~ River Road ~ Benzonia ~ now the Benzie Area Historical Museum

"The old church building, in common with just about all the church buildings of the land, was not used solely for Sunday morning services. Sunday School, the Christian Endeavor meeting, mid-week prayer meetings (remember them?), and other meetings of religious significance [were also held]. For many years it was the site of high school and Benzonia Academy commencement week activities. Concerts, lectures, and even dramatics have been presented from its rostrum. The dining room in the basement (Sunday School rooms on Sundays) was often the scene of community banquets and programs. And for years, those never to be forgotten Christmas Eve programs with the ceiling-high balsam tree glowing with live candles and bedecked with trimmings of the most inflammable material imaginable. Why the church didn't burn down every Christmas Eve is a matter to ponder and be thankful for."

Case

St. Ann Catholic Church ~ Frankfort ~ c. 1909

"St. Ann's Catholic Church . . . began in 1885 with Rev. Father Kotman, priest. The first building was constructed in 1895 and Saint Ann's was established as a parish in 1915."

Bixby
Benzie County Record Patriot

Congregational Church ~ Thompsonville ~ 1929

Elberta Methodist Church

"Religious services were first held in homes or by any other ways or means at hand. Open air meetings were supplemented by services held in the old log schoolhouse and later in Temperance Hall."

"In the early days before radio and television, a great deal of the social life of the village eminated from the Methodist Church. Easter programs, Christmas plays, and other forms of entertainment were a continuing thing. Dinners put on by the ladies of the church were always a social event and a way to make a little money for the good cause. . . ."

Blacklock

The Indian Mission ~ Honor

"The church was a Methodist Church of the Wilderness, located in Honor before 1910."

Bailey

First church and log school house in the lumbering town of Aral ~ c.1880s

Aral School ~ teacher and students c.1906

Barber Hall Recitation Building ~ Benzonia Academy

Benzonia Academy ~ Barber Hall is on the right

"In the winter of 1860 and '61, there were thirteen families in the settlement [of Benzonia]. In 1860 the first district school was opened . . . in a part of the dwelling-house of John Bailey. . . . Soon afterward a log building was erected and used for school and church purposes."

The Traverse Region

"The founding fathers were men from Oberlin College. . . . Their faith was in the revealed religion as expounded by the Congregational Church . . . so they founded the town of Benzonia . . . and in 1863, the new college opened its doors and went into operation: Grand Traverse College, newest and tiniest of the educational institutions of a struggling new state."

"By the end of the 1890's . . . Benzonia College could exist no longer. . . . The college was voted out of its existence, and in its place there was a preparatory school, Benzonia Academy. . . . This change from college to academy took place in the year 1900."

Catton

Chemistry Class ~ Benzonia College ~ 1893

"Barber Hall contained a study hall, 4 or 5 classrooms, a chapel, a diminutive library, and a room which passed as laboratory and museum for the physical sciences. This room was somewhat primitive, there was no running water, and there was no gas for Bunsen burners, but there was a zinc-topped table and there were shelves behind glass doors along one wall, containing instructive specimens. I can dimly remember seeing a row of rocks, representing Heaven knows what, and a glass jar full of alcohol containing a human fetus. There was also a skeleton in one corner. As a center for instruction in physics, chemistry, and zoology it was grotesquely inadequate but it was more than the college had ever had to offer before."

Catton

Girl's Basketball Team ~ Benzonia Academy ~ 1910 – 1911

". . . that academy lasted eighteen years altogether."

Catton

Benzonia—Beulah Public School ~ Benzonia ~ c. 1916

"The Benzonia-Beulah Public School is one that any village can justly feel proud. The school is housed in an attractive, modern, and beautifully located building over-looking Crystal Lake. The farm boys and girls are transported from the outlying districts by large buses and private vehicles, numbering 300. The standards of scholarship, athletics, and school loyalty are of the highest order, which is an inspiration to all who come there. Its graduates are admitted to any institution of higher learning in the state without an examination and the past records show that 98 percent of all its graduates have entered one of these institutions."

Benzie County Information Bureau

Thompsonville School ~ c.1910

"One clung to little privileges. There was a flagpole, and it was a major perquisite to be allowed to run the flag up early in the day and take it down before the bus came. There was no patriotism in this, just ritual, for which we were well conditioned by the church. As I grew stronger, I tried to see how high I could climb on the pole and made it up two of the three sections, as I recall. . . . Another perquisite was dusting the blackboard erasers. The felt would clog up with chalk dust, and the way to clean the erasers was to take them out and pound them against the porch or the side of the schoolhouse until the dust was out."

Stadtfeld

Thompsonville Basketball Team ~ 1913

Drake School House 1891-1943 ~ Platte Township District No. 2 ~ c.1920s

"One of my happiest years was the fifth grade. . . . I . . . had some standing with my fellows and had managed to get a seat near a window. On spring afternoons, I could levitate myself out that window to all the mysteries I knew. . . . Our imaginations were rooted there in what we saw, and we wanted to be part of it, to grow up naturally, to share the scene that other youngsters would look down on from those windows. It was such a logical evolution, such a natural step. Perhaps that was what made the community so stable for all those years, and what made the break so severe when it became impossible for us to be part of that pastoral picture we had looked down as children." *This building is currently owned by the Benzie Area Historical Society and was built in 1891 and closed in 1943.*

Stadtfeld

What a wonderful way to combine studying with play on a beautiful snowy day ~ across from Drake School ~ a one-room school house in Platte Township c.1930s

Elberta School ~ Kindergarten through 12th Grade

"The big school at the corner of Steele and George M. Streets in what is now Elberta was constructed in 1870. It was first two stories and of wood, later it was raised one story and the entire first story constructed of brick. In 1906 three stories were added as an addition on the south side and a steam heating plant installed to heat the entire building. . . . This building was dismantled in the early 1960s."

Blacklock

Corner Grove School students ~ Gilmore Township ~ 1909-1910

Schoolhouse at Honor

Honor High School Basketball Champions of District 25
Class D Third Place Regional District at Petoskey

Bendon High School

"Our truant officer entertained some of our citizens by reading the law. The result was a better attendance at school last week." *February 24, 1898*

"A special meeting will be held Saturday night to determine whether we shall have a one or two room school next year." *June 1, 1916*

Benzie Banner

"We memorized multiplication tables, all the words in the old green spellers, the songs in the song books. . . . We learned to diagram sentences and to get the hell out of the building in under three minutes in case anyone ever dropped a forbidden match on one of those tinder-dry, oil-saturated floors, because the whole shebang would have gone up like a Roman candle."

Stadtfeld

Long building with three doors housed Benzie County Normal, the Frankfort Library, and a meeting room for scouts and other groups ~ c.1909

"Education has played an important part in the life of Frankfort. In the very early years, a borrowed building on Main Street served as the first school. In 1868, a building 25 feet by 50 feet was constructed at the north end of Sixth Street. An addition was soon needed and the building then housed the school, the jail, the library, and when needed, the county court.

The building on Sixth Street continued to be used for library, jail, and community activities. In 1908, the Benzie County Normal was established in this building for the purpose of preparing young people for a career in teaching. The first class graduated in 1909 and the final class in 1960. Six hundred and forty students were graduated and received teaching certificates in those 51 years."

Bixby & Sandman

Frankfort School ~ Kindergarten through High School

"In 1894 a large imposing red brick building was opened for school. . . "
                                                        Bixby & Sandman

A well appointed school office with a roll-top desk, Edison Mimeograph case, and typewriter ~ Frankfort ~ 1891

Notice those computations on the blackboard ~ no computers here! ~ Frankfort School classroom ~ 1891

String Ensemble ~ Frankfort School presentation ~ 1891

Frankfort High School Pole Vault Competition

Frankfort High School Girl's Drill Team ~ 1910

"The pins competition was actually an Olympic event at that time."

Laarman

Proud cheerleaders in new skirts, letter sweaters, and saddle shoes ~ Frankfort ~ 1948

Posing before a performance ~ Frankfort High School Band ~ Fall 1950

Michigan Avenue ~ Benzonia

"Our town was different. It was put there by men who believed that there was going to be a future, and who built for it. When they looked about them, they saw people instead of trees; what was going on, as far as they were concerned, was not so much the reduction of pine logs to sawn timber as the foundation of a human society."

Catton

The village blacksmith ~ Benzonia ~ 1898

". . . The smith, a mighty man is he,
With large and sinewy hands;
And the muscles of his brawny
arms
Are strong as iron bands."
Longfellow

An important man for every community was the blacksmith. He made
and repaired a variety of items including horseshoes, tools, and hardware.

We fix anything! ~ the Fix-It Shop ~ Benzonia ~ c.1940s

"To be sure, there are the necessary business houses, bank, post-office, garage, merchants in every line; telephone, electric service for power and light (from a harnessing of the Betsey River.) In spite of these modern aspects of the village life, however, the appeal which Benzonia makes most strongly to the resident or resorter is that which challenges his love of the quiet, beautiful, and natural."

Benzie County Information Bureau

Enjoying a stroll in downtown Beulah ~ c.1910

"For a full third of a century, 1899–1932, Benzonia and Beulah carried on as a single incorporated municipality. . . . Late in the 1920s, . . . a feeling grew that possibly it would be better . . . if the village should separate into two corporate municipal entities. . . . Late in 1931, . . . Beulah and Benzonia were finally separate entities . . . and time has pretty much justified the separation. . . . Now as never before Beulah on its 'Shining, Glorious Shore' and Benzonia, 'a good place' on its hill top site, continue to be one and inseparable in all the intangible values that make life well worth the living in what is still 'The Twin Villages.'"

Case

Beulah ~ 1913

"Have you ever been there? It's such a grand place to spend your vacation, with so many miles of shore line, and so many places to go with your boats, for your picnic dinner, pretty bays, and wooded glens where the spring brooks drop down into the lake. Parks, groves, beautiful drives, walks, and in fact everything to make your vacation as well as your permanent summer home the most ideal in the state."

Benzie County Information Bureau

An early Beulah business ~ Gibbs Drug Store ~ c.1899

Crystal Lake waterfront ~ ~ aftermath of the lowering of Crystal Lake in 1873

"Before the advent of rail or highway transportation, transportation of goods and people by water was about the only means available to the early settlers. . . . It would be a boon to the country if a navigable waterway could be established from Crystal Lake to the Frankfort waterfront. And when Mr. Archibald Jones came to Benzonia in 1872, he thought he saw possibilities along this line.

He would build a canal between Crystal Lake and Betsie River. In making preliminary plans for the canal a vital matter in its success was wholly neglected. No surveys were made as to the differences in the water levels of Crystal Lake and Lake Michigan.

In 1873 the canal was dug, opened, and the result was pure catastrophe. For days the water poured out of Crystal Lake from its higher level, and so once again the only water connection between the lake and Betsie River was the little meandering outlet stream.

However, the lowering of the lake created a beautiful beach and sites for the future village of Beulah. In short, it was the making of Crystal Lake as one of the more attractive and popular inland lakes of all Michigan."

Case

Crystal Lake Boy's Camp at the Crystal Lake Outlet

From roadside to a thriving business ~ original Cherry Hut ~ Beulah ~ 1922

Famously delicious cherry products ~ Cherry Hut

Main Street ~ Thompsonville

Before the railroads, "Thompsonville was a small town, was fairly new in the country. They used to call it Beecher. . . . There were 5 saloons in a town that had a population of about 500 people. The Pickway Handle Company was there, the National Basket Company was there. That was in my time. I've hauled logs in there. Five saloons and I think two grocery stores. You need more whiskey than you did groceries, you know."

Overlease

Supplying all your needs ~ Wareham General Store ~ Thompsonville

Oval Dish Company ~ Thompsonville ~ c.1901

"In the days before containers made of paper, plastics, ceramics, or other ingeniously contrived materials took their place, wooden containers of all sorts and sizes were widely used. So a factory was set up which employed crews like this and turned out by the millions all sorts of wooden containers, especially butter bowls."

Case

Piqua Handle Works ~ Thompsonville

"The Piqua Handle Company started in Thompsonville around 1910. . . .
They made all sizes and kinds of hardwood handles, also jointed wood poles
for pup tents in World War I. At the peak of its operations it employed over
100 men and was Thompsonville's main employer at that time."

Gibbs

Julius Hale's Barber Shop ~ Thompsonville

"Shave and a haircut, two bits."
1899 song by
Charles Hale

Spring Water: fill your thermos bottle here ~ Main Street ~ Honor

"For upwards of twenty years after the railroads made their advent into Honor (1895), things there went along in a wonderful way. . . . The going and coming of trains, the intense activity at the mill yards, and the noises incident hereto, in the wintertime the creaking sleighs loaded high with prime logs passing along the Main Street all contributed to the liveliness that was Honor. . . ."

"Inevitably the mill . . . deforested the hills and valleys of Platte River, and by 1915 they were barren of everything but stumps and tinder dry slashings. With the forests went the mill and with the mill went the railroads."

"The mill gone, the railroads gone, the county seat gone, many of the people gone, Honor might have deteriorated into a state of innocuous desuetude . . .but not so. Beautiful Platte River still flows, and the surrounding hills . . . still stand and are again clothed with verdures. But best of all, the people, its citizens, have not let their little village die. It lives and grows and prospers because its people have found life well worth the effort in the Platte River Valley."

Case

Clean, clear ice was easy to find in most Benzie County lakes ~ Honor 1910

". . . ice was cut with a handsaw. Sometimes the ice was 2 foot thick, cut in blocks 2 foot square. Carland had an ice house about 70' by 40' that was filled to the top with ice during February. The ice was put in tiers, 12 blocks high with saw dust from maple and birch packed on the bottom, sides, and top. Two feet of sawdust was used to keep the ice from melting during the hot summer months."

Anderson

Weaver Bros. ~ the best meat market in Honor ~ get your pig's feet here ~ try them!

Modeling those stunning hats ~ no well dressed woman would be without one! ~ Honor

The Village of Lake Ann was incorporated in 1893

Lake Ann "covers a relatively short span in comparison to the long and rich history which preceded the arrival of the white settlers. It had been a land of swamps and forests where there were mastodons, mammoths, peccaries, and the musk ox; it was the bottom of the ocean and the land of the glaciers."

Brosier

On July 4th, 1897 . . . in the village of Lake Ann, which was quite a thriving mill and manufacturing town, no special celebration had been planned. . . . As it turned out, Lake Ann had its own massive display of fireworks that day and it was not firecrackers, Roman candles, nor skyrockets. . . . At 1:30 in the afternoon . . . a fire was discovered in or near the engine room of the Habbeler sawmill. . . . Almost at once the mill was on fire, and almost at once the fire spread across town . . . Of the estimated eighty-eight buildings in town on the morning of that day, the setting sun, through a murky haze of residual smoke, shone on only sixteen.

The village never fully recovered from its ordeal. Its mill was gone, its stave and head factory was gone, many of its homes and stores were gone, and a portion of its then nearly 1,000 population moved away. But its spirit survived this and two subsequent fires . . ." and it is now once again a thriving village.

Case

In appreciation for Lake Ann's help in naming Frankfort the Benzie County seat in 1894, Frankfort chartered this train to bring a Lake Ann delegation to town for a celebration ~ April 3, 1895

Bird's eye view of South Frankfort, which became the Village of Elberta in 1911

Main Street Elberta ~ a welcoming town and a great place to "fill up"

Elberta "has the large transfer business of the Ann Arbor Railroad, and has a large water frontage which is an ideal site for factories, it having both rail and water frontage for shipping. Good stocks are kept in all the stores and the surrounding country finds a ready market and abundant supplies."

Benzie County Information Bureau 1916

"The late Paul Rose shipped thousand of bushels of the choicest peaches and other fruits, and such a large proportion was of the Elberta Variety, that the name was changed from South Frankfort to Elberta, and the seeing of that large fine peach will always remind you of the Benzie County town that ships thousands of bushels of the finest fruit with flavor."

Benzie County Information Bureau 1916

These early containers were used for shipping, rain barrels, and storage ~ Matzinger and Hancock Cooper Shop ~ Elberta

Tie up to the old hitching post and shop ~ Glarum & Classens ~ South Frankfort ~ c.1880s

"In the year 1896 or 1897, they commenced the construction of the finest store building constructed in the village . . . a large grocery department and the office made up the south side of the store while the north side held the largest stock of dry goods, clothing and shoes and other items this side of Traverse City or Cadillac. In fact, it was said that people as far as the Traverse City area came to the big sales which Glarum and Classens were famous for, in spite of the stocks available at home and the difficulties of travel in those early days."

Blacklock

Elberta Packing Company ~ Elberta ~ 1936-1969

"The Elberta Packing Company was organized in 1936 to can cherries then expanded to process other fruits and vegetables. . . . The company employed around 200 people in the cherry canning season."

Blacklock

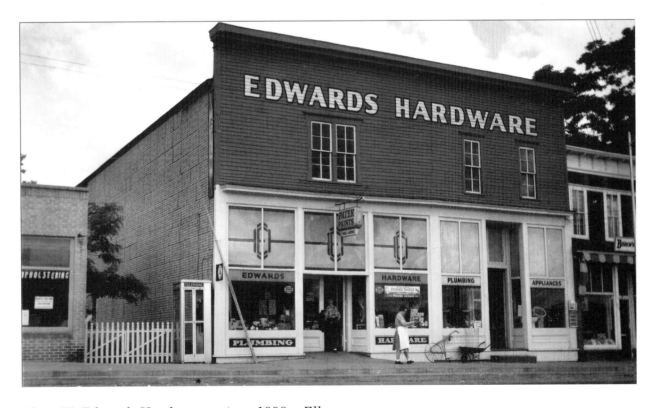

Geo. W. Edwards Hardware ~ since 1898 ~ Elberta

Heavy duty pulling power ~ Frankfort

Call the City Dray for your hauling needs ~ Elberta

"Almost every place of business such as grocery stores and general merchandise had their own delivery rigs, others made a business of 'Draying.'"

Blacklock

Frankfort Iron Works ~ 1883

"One of the first developments, as a result of the harbor entrance improvements by the United States Government starting in 1867, was the construction and operation of a huge Iron Works in South Frankfort, now Elberta. The Frankfort Iron Works, with main office in Detroit, Michigan, was established and work began on the construction of the Blast Furnace in 1869. . . .The location of the furnace in South Frankfort gave this village the largest and most extensive manufacturing works in Benzie County during its existence. . . .Fifteen tons of iron were manufactured on that first day, and the ultimate capacity of the furnaces reached forty tons a day."

Blacklock

Frankfort panorama taken at the top of Fourth Street, with the Upton home in the foreground ~ c.1900 ~ the widow's walk was a convenient source of "air conditioning" on hot, humid days, and also provided access for the chimney sweep

"Frankfort has many fine homes which are rented for the season, also numerous rooms are rented, which are convenient to the hotels and restaurants. The hotels are located near Lake Michigan, and it is only a short walk to the wonderful sand bathing beach where people spend so many happy hours. The beautiful sunsets from the beach and bluffs will linger long in your memory, and you will often be found quoting the Frankfort sunsets."

Benzie County Information Bureau 1916

Exchanging the latest news and picking up supplies at the hardware store ~ or for a quick visit to the doctor's office, which is just above the store ~ Frankfort

H. Woodward & Son ~ Main Street, Frankfort ~ was located on Betsie Bay, which enabled both front and back door deliveries ~ dirt roads and board sidewalks were still common

Main Street, Frankfort ~ 1916

"I like it here ~ this is a real town."
Anonymous

Sporting the classy hats, caps, and shoes from Glarum and Classens ~ 1908

Watchmaker working his trade above the bustling street below

As two-story buildings were added to the community, the upstairs rooms were used for a variety of purposes, such as offices for watchmakers, tailors, doctors, dentists, apartments, etc. In some cases they were used for dances, club meetings, and even basketball!

Frankfort's early Mineral Springs at Butler's Mill ~ 1889

"Frankfort's Mineral Springs was developed by accident in 1881 when D. B. Butler, encouraged by success in the Manistee area, decided to drill for salt. . . . Drillers at Frankfort expected to reach a heavy body of rock salt at a depth of 2,000 feet. Instead, the well produced mineral water, under intense pressure, at an estimated initial flow of 8,000 barrels daily. . . ."

In the early 1900s when the Royal Frontenac Hotel was still standing on the west side of town, . . . the hotel's bathhouse . . . had its water piped down from the mineral springs as a kind of health bath. There were booths and a charge of twenty-five cents was made for the privilege of bathing there."

Bixby & Sandman

Mineral Springs Park ~ c. 1895

"For four seasons (April to November), I worked at the J. C. Pomeroy Bottling Works in Frankfort where mineral water was bottled in quart bottles from the 2000 foot deep mineral spring. Bottling 32 quarts a day was quite a day's work."

Henry Michael (Seabury)

A familiar landmark welcoming you to Frankfort ~ the Marine Gateway ~ c.1932

"It was Joe Winkler's idea in 1925 to construct a lasting monument to the Ann Arbor Carferries . . . and despite the fact that it has been moved once and taken down for re-modeling another time, the Frankfort Gateway Arch remains a tribute to the ships that once sailed out of the Port City."

Bixby & Sandman

Relaxing on the cannon ~ Frankfort ~ 1922

"For nearly a century, a Civil War cannon has guarded the Frankfort Harbor in its own silent and symbolic way. The cannon came to Frankfort in the late 1800s from Buffalo, New York. By the late 1800s—about the time of the Spanish American War—this type of cannon was definitely obsolete and those that were not shipped back to the foundries for recycling were readily available to any community which might desire one and had the proper connections with whoever its Congressman may have been. . . . At one time, a small pyramid of cannon balls gave the touch of authenticity to the old gun but one by one they have disappeared."

Bixby & Sandman

Armour Company Fruit Preserving Station

Some people will recognize this structure as the site of the Armour Company Fruit Preserving Station, or the Frankfort Canning Factory, or the Pontiac Millwork Company, or finally the Smokestack.

A general store for all your needs, or order from our catalogue ~ 1901

Look at those *meat prices! ~ Ferris-Jackson Store ~ c.1950*

Bendon ~ Inland Township

"The truly pioneering experiences . . . were exchanged for the comparative civilized conditions of a populated village. Mrs. Edwards remembered what a thrill it was for her when she could actually see from her home the home of a neighbor and could see the lights come on in the village as the lengthening shadows cast by the western bluffs deepened into darkness."

Case

Forging a Spirit of Community

Creating a new road ~ Beulah Hill ~ 1909

The need for roads was clear. Communities in Benzie County were isolated from one another. In order to create this road on the Beulah Hill, workers used shovels to remove the dirt. As earth was excavated, it was loaded in dump carts and conveyed down the hill on a wooden track. Carts were returned uphill by a team of mules. Strenuous work, but the men were up to the task!

Hard, hard work merits a short break to refresh from that "little brown jug" ~ Stratton Hill ~ south of Elberta

Using teams of horses to prepare the road bed

Improved roads were often constructed close to the railroad tracks. It took ten horse power to pull the heavily weighted equipment needed to grade the road bed.

Improvement meant sidewalks in town, so now a lady's skirts and shoes were protected from mud ~ laying the first concrete sidewalk in South Frankfort ~ c.1894

U.S. Mail rural delivery RFD #2 ~ 1909

"The mail was carried on horseback in the summer and on sleds and snow shoes in the winter over a trail or foot path marked by blazed trees."

Seabury

"There was a post office at Herring Creek, and a man named Averil was postmaster. In 1850 that office was removed to Benzonia. . . . The post office was brought from Herring Creek by boat and once for a brief time the office and postmaster entirely disappeared under water by the upsetting of the boat."

The Traverse Region

Beulah Post Office ~ c.1910

"The arrival of the mail was considered a great event, and was the subject of conversation for days after."

Seabury

"The Frankfort post office was established in 1860 and re-established in 1867. . . . Among [the postmaster's] duties being that of carrying the mail from Benzonia to Frankfort on foot."

Howard

"There are 17 rural mail routes in Benzie County, covering nearly 250 miles."

Benzie County Patriot
April 1911

Wooden planked bridge leading to a log-based corduroy roadway ~ a hazard to horses due to loose logs that could roll and shift

River Road Bridge over Betsie River near Benzonia

"One night, two fellows sped away from a dance hall and were soon followed by a motor-cycle policeman. They turned onto a corduroy road which proved to be too bumpy for the policeman and he had to slow down. The laughing fellows got away."

Clark

"Modern" improvements continued to come to Benzie County ~ linemen, a goundman, and a skinner (on wagon) working to provide electricity

Benzie County Power Company ~ Homestead Dam

"Prior to 1893, the only source of light in the nighttime (with the exception of that received from the moon and the stars) in the county was wax or tallow candles and even the warm glow from an open fireplace. To be sure there were kerosene lamps in many homes and the lanterns for cellar, woodshed, barn chores, and after dark walking along the country roads. . . . The first glimmering of the dawn from this dark age in the county came to Frankfort in 1893 when . . . a steam powered electric plant [was installed]."

Case

Main Street ~ Thompsonville ~ 1904

"In the 1890s, Thompsonville was, for quite a few years, the most lighted up town that can be imagined. Street lights and porch lights of the homes seemed to be aglow at all times even during the daylight hours. During the evening hours, the windows of the homes radiated a warm glow of lights from within indicating that almost every room in the house was lighted by electricity."

Case

Aftermath of an ice storm ~ Bear Lake

"It happened on George Washington's birthday, February 22, 1922. . . .
About the most vivid memories that most people have of that historic night
was the incessant booming, cracking and crashing of branches and whole
trees that fell under the ever increasing weight of ice as it built up, inches
thick. Lights went out in homes wired with electricity; telephones went
dead; and by morning it seemed as though every home and building was an
isolated island in a frozen sea of shimmering ice."

Case

High wire workers without a net ~ installing electric and telephone lines is dangerous work

Soon telephones became an important part of daily life ~ Frank-fort's first telephone office opened December 4, 1899

"Number please" ~ Beulah telephone office ~ c.1940

". . . one would call the operator and ask her to connect you with the party you cared to talk to. They were the first to know the gossip around Frankfort."

Anderson

"This good old world will lose something bright and beautiful, something that cannot be duplicated or equaled when the last telephone operator takes off her head set, climbs down off her stool, and turns everything over to some miserable electronic contraption which has not heart, soul, or spirit."

Case

Early medical office

Medical care has always been needed. A good doctor gave such care by making house calls, or by attending to his patients in his in-home office. Nurses provided maternity help, as did midwives. Care for the sick was a labor of love and was aided by the willing hands of family, friends and neighbors.

An in-home doctor's office ~ 1919

Dr. Frank La Rue and his wife worked as a team for many years - delivering babies, performing surgery, and caring for those who were injured ~ Elberta ~1890s-1940s

Anna Markham Memorial Hospital ~ Frankfort

"Babies seemed to always come in 'bunches'. Many times our little nursery was filled to capacity."

Ena Kraft Jackson, R.N.

Paul Oliver Memorial Hospital ~ the first hospital to adequately serve all of Benzie County ~ c.1950s

Paul Oliver Memorial Hospital replaced the need for home care facilities.

Protecting Our Freedom

The freighter Lawrence went aground "on the shore two miles south of Point Betsey on Thanksgiving eve, 1898, while the captain [Harrison Miller] was in charge of the life-saving station at the point. Hearing the distress whistle, the captain and his crew started up the shore with the surf boat and the breeches buoy. No object could be seen three feet ahead. The denseness of the snow in the air can be understood from the fact that twenty-three inches of it fell during that night. Hence the vessel could not be seen, and the life-savers had only the sound of the whistle to guide them.

A part of the Lawrence's crew had tried to make shore in the lifeboat, but it swamped and one man drowned. Captain Miller found the dead body, while members of the crew picked up the others and took them back to Point Betsey Station where Captain Miller's wife and children gave them hot coffee and food and put them to bed, swathed in blankets. Meantime the Captain had shot a line out toward the vessel. A terrific wind was blowing, and in addition, he had only the sound of the whistle from which to judge in what general direction to shoot. No sign came from the crew that they had observed the line, so he tried again. The second line was lost, and the Captain ordered the men to pull in the first one. As they pulled, the line held fast, showing it caught something. Then the whistle on the vessel again began to blow. It quickly became evident that the line had fallen over the whistle cord, so that when the lifeguard pulled on it they blew the whistle. This attracted the attention of the freighter's crew, and in almost no time at all the breeches buoy was in operation and 14 men on the doomed vessel were taken off. The vessel was a total wreck, being pounded to pieces by the heavy surf."

Howard

Life Saving Station and Betsie Bay ~ c.1880

U.S. Life Saving Station in South Frankfort (Elberta)

"Note the small square look-out tower on top of the Station where the crew stood watches 24 hours a day. They also patrolled the beach south and north of Frankfort for two and one-half miles. There was a clock they had to punch on a post on either end of the patrol. The last man towards morning would bring the punched card into the station and also put another in its place. The following morning, the Skipper would look it over to see if it was properly punched. If not, that man was not allowed to leave the station grounds for 30 days."

Anderson

They had to go out, they didn't always come back ~ Life Saving Crew ~ c.1907

It was a spectacular drill ~ U.S. Life Saving crew practicing a "controlled roll" ~ Elberta

"In the early days, these gallant men in their small boats put to sea in foul and fair weather and rowed many miles to aid a ship and crew in distress, etc. Often they would venture outside when tugs and larger craft refused to brave the weather. On various holidays they would put on a spectacular drill while the water front was lined with townsfolk and visitors."

Frederickson

U.S. Life Saving Station ~ Point Betsie ~ Frankfort

The Life Saving Station at Pt. Betsie was built in 1875 at a cost of $3,000. The station was located on the shores of Lake Michigan. A typical week for the men living and working at the station was filled with drills and patrols. This readied these brave men to risk their lives during bad storms in the Manitou Passage.

Enjoying a beautiful day on the beach at Point Betsie

Point Betsie Lighthouse is the oldest standing structure in Benzie County. It was built in 1858 at a cost of $5,000. Point Betsie marks the southern entrance to the Manitou Passage, which is seven miles wide from South Manitou Island to the mainland — Sleeping Bear Point. The navigable deep channel is only a mile across, but it is the most dangerous passage on the Great Lakes. The area was once a vital maritime shipping channel. However, because of the many shoals and storms, the Manitou Passage could be dangerous to navigate. To aid ships in all kinds of weather, the light at Point Betsie is housed 52 ft. above Lake Michigan and has a range of 27.5 miles.

Point Betsie Coast Guard wives marching for the vote in 1914 ~ women too, wanted a voice in community decisions

First all-female jury in Benzie County ~ 1919

Civil War Veterans Fife and Drum Corp ~ "It is well that war is so terrible; else we should grow too fond of it." General Robert E. Lee

Reunion of Civil War Soldiers in 1889 ~ Honor ~ Civil War 1861-1865

"One time the Grand Army of the Republic held a mammoth encampment in Honor and for several days a vacant lot at the west edge of the village was white with tents among which the veterans, in their blue uniforms, brass buttons, and black campaign hats moved and exchanged wondrous tales of mighty deeds of valor performed in putting down the late Rebellion against the Union."

Case

Sending our boys to war ~ first volunteers from Frankfort ~ WWI 1914-1918

Keep the Home Fires Burning

"They were summoned from the hillside,
They were summoned from the glen,
And the country found them ready
At the stirring call for men.
Let no tears add to their hardship,
As the soldiers pass along,
And although your heart is breaking,
Make it sing this cheery song.
Refrain:
Keep the Homefires burning,
While your hearts are yearning
Though your lads are far away
They dream of home.
There's a silver lining
Through the dark cloud shining,
Turn the dark cloud inside out,
Till the boys come home.

Army Song Book

Off to war

Returning Veterans

Proud of our service men ~ World War I

Women doing their part ~ Nurses WWII ~ Italy ~ 1943

The nurses were in every sense at war, side by side with the men. The difference was that they fought hard to preserve life while everyone around them was bent on taking it.

USS Oahu officers and crew ~ 1944 ~ WW II 1941-1945

"During World War II, a temporary armistice occurred in Italy on Easter Sunday of 1944. . . . 'The thing wasn't planned in Washington, London, or Berlin so far as is known. Probably the commanding officer on either side knew nothing of it beforehand. It was just planned and carried out by a bunch of boys and young men who, through no fault of their own and with little to say in the matter, were pitted against each other in mortal combat in Italy on Easter morning.

For a matter of two hours on that Sabbath morning, all firing ceased, death took a holiday, while German boys and American boys joined in a common Easter Service around a common alter. God in Heaven must have looked down on that death strewn hillside and wept. All the longings of battle weary men for peace among the nations, all the ultimate futility of wars, all the hopes for a lasting foundation of good will towards men were bound up in the eloquence of those two hours of peace, two hours in which hate and savage brutality were replaced by forces infinitely greater. Two hours in which man acknowledged his brotherhood to man. If for two hours, why not for two days, two years, two centuries?"

Case

From here to there ~ a journey starts with a first step

. . . and then came the all important horse ~ teachers on their way to school discussing the day's lesson plan

Between 1865 and 1915, the horse and buggy was the most popular mode of short-distance transportation. During that time, horseback riding was less common and required more specific skill than driving a buggy. Buggies could cost as little as $25 to $50, and could easily be driven by women or children.

Passengers waiting for the ship on the Frankfort Dock ~ 1913

"With the improved . . . facilities, Frankfort became known as a summer resort, and each season hundreds of families came here to enjoy the climate and natural beauty."

Seabury

Steamer Puritan in channel ~ Frankfort

"After the channel to Betsie Bay was dredged, many steam boats, passenger boats, along with sail vessels, began to enter Frankfort Harbor. . . . People came here from Chicago and other cities to escape the summer heat. The ships all carried freight and other supplies [for the local] merchants."

Anderson

Sailing was a popular way to enjoy the inland lakes

Riding around Crystal Lake on the Pathfinder "taxi"

"Cruising by water before the auto was the only way to see much of the scenery and enjoy a good rest at the same time. Stops were made at resorts around Crystal Lake and brought [people] to and fro into Beulah. Entertainment awaited."

Frederickson

From steam power to gas power ~ out for a ride in their Horseless Carriage ~ Benzonia ~ c.1910

"So we had seen the automobile and there was no way for the most imaginative man to see that here was the perfect symbol of the new era . . ."

Catton

Maneuvering down the sandy road on those thin tires was a challenge!

"I remember one summer day, early in the [20th] century, when a ball game was in progress, and an automobile came chug-chugging along and drew up on the grass back of the right field foul line. An automobile was a rare sight in our county; hardly anybody had enough money to buy and support one, and the sandy roads provided almost impossible driving conditions. . . .The automobile stopped to see the game, and the game stopped to see the automobile."

Catton

Early roads were extremely hard on wheels and tires ~ 1904

"As we grew older and cars entered our lives, an old 'one' came into our possession. It might be more accurate to say it possessed us as we were always tinkering with the beast. It was said all you needed to repair 'it' was a pair of pliers and a roll of baling wire and that's about the way we tackled the job - Read this and weep - gasoline was about 10–15 cents a gallon, but we mixed it with a third kerosene to make it cheaper."

Barnard

A Place for all Seasons

Enjoying the view from gigantic Lake Michigan ice formations ~ 1922

"Winter is our season up north. It claims us. We have to claim it, like an undertow, if you fight it, it'll wear you out. 'Just submit,' a friend said one winter. And I did. And it worked. . . . We feel winter here, before it comes, with those shifts in wind coming across the lake. We can feel it even in June, but as soon as school starts in September, we can actually smell it on the wind. By the time the big lake storms come in October and November, we are feeling it daily."

Stocking

What is this contraption?"

How creative! A motor and an airplane propeller mounted on runners ~ and it really worked!

Winter fun on a Beulah "mountain"

Here I go!!

I want my own sled! ~ waiting patiently for a ride through the snow ~ Beulah

Family fun ~ sliding down Hefferon Hill ~ Frankfort ~ c.1945

"One of the best sledding hills in the area was Hefferon Hill which is on Michigan Avenue. In those days, the streets were not sanded so your sled could really zip along. The younger or less daring sledders would start at the bottom to middle of the hill while the dare devils went right to the top. The competition was to see how far you could slide, with Main Street being the ultimate goal. A little extra weight on the sled was a big advantage."

Beidler

The design and speed of the jumper varied with the ingenuity of the builder!

"It's believed that jumpers originated in the Scandinavian countries. A jumper was a sturdy homemade affair consisting of a seat on an upright piece of wood that was attached to a curved runner with a metal surface. One sat on a jumper at the top of the hill, hung onto both sides of the seat, then pushed off with the feet. The feet were held up in front ready to drag as necessary for turns and stops. The older kids added to their fun by making moguls to jump. The younger ones had to maneuver around them by dragging one foot or the other, and if we weren't successful, we crashed!

Jumpers were so popular that they were carried to school to use at recess, then taken home after school so they could be used again before dark."

Clark

Bringing out the snowshoes for a trek through the woods

"One day that first winter [1859], when the snow was deep, father went out into the woods. He saw some very huge tracks in the snow. He went back to the cabin, got in a lot of wood, barred the door securely, and said 'There must be some awful big animal in the woods.' He had seen its tracks, but nothing appeared and a few days later a neighbor came along walking on snowshoes. They were the tracks he had seen!" *Anna Rebecca Edwards* quote

Case

*Early rope tow in Benzonia which later became the first
rope tow at Buck Hills ~ Thompsonville*

"In the 1950s waitress trays were used for sliding. These later became the commercial snow disks."

Laarman

Elberta Mountain Ski Park ~ c.1950s

"Ragnar Robertson came to Elberta in the 1920s. He had migrated to the United States from his native Norway. . . . In the early 1940s, Robertson began to try to interest local people in the building of a ski jump as he had found a natural spot for one in Elberta Hills. The Elberta Village Council decided to try 'some development in the winter sports field.'. . . In 1951 on February 10th and 11th, in spite of a warm spell, the first Winter Sports Festival was held with great success. . . . The ski-jumping exhibitions drew almost every ski-jumper of known ability in the Lower Peninsula of Michigan. . . . Highlight of the festival was toboggan jumping off the smaller ski jump with a jump of 90 feet being executed. . . ."

Blacklock

Unfortunately, due to snow and temperature variations, this area was never developed further and was eventually closed.

Getting ready to grab the tow rope for that ride to the top of the mountain ~ and then came that invigorating downhill run! ~ Buck Hills (later Crystal Mountain) ~ Thompsonville ~ c.1950s

Family-owned Crystal Mountain owes its establishment to a group of dedicated local citizens, each of whom had an immense passion for skiing. It was this passion that led to the development of Buck Hills ski area in Michigan's Benzie County. Buck Hills featured two rope tows and a small warming hut. It was originally purchased by a group of investors. In 1960 new owners named it Crystal Mountain.

"We did a good deal of skiing in a makeshift sort of way. All of the skis were home-made - a local carpenter would produce a pair for a modest sum – and they lacked modern refinements; there was simply a leather strap on each ski to put your toe through, with nothing to go round your heel and bind you firmly to the skis. Maneuvers that are taken for granted by present-day skiers were utterly beyond our reach, but we could go swinging down the open slopes at a great rate, and glide across country in fine style, and since we did not know that we lacked anything we were completely satisfied."

Catton

207

Lining up for the start of the race ~ a good time on the ice

Ice boating on Crystal Lake ~ 1943 ~ the ice boat can reach at least four times the speed of the wind propelling it

"There have been years when the whole surface of the lake [Crystal] was a gigantic natural skating rink and ice boating speedway. One year, it must have been in the early 1920s, this condition prevailed for a week or two. The ice was as clear and smooth as a pane of glass and thick without a flake of snow on its whole surface. . . . In addition to the blood tingling delight of unlimited skating during those wonderful days there was the sport of driving your car out on the lake, attaching to it a stout line, attaching to the line a queue of skaters, and then all go rolling and gliding along with now and then a crack-the-whip maneuver to liven things up a bit."

Case

Visiting the ice fishing shanties on Crystal Lake ~ Beulah

Don't forget to make the hole larger than the fish you expect to spear

"Winter fishing through the ice on the lake has always been popular and there was a time, soon after the advent and discovery of smelt in the lake, when one could hardly see the ice for the hundreds of fish shanties scattered all over from end to end and side to side of the lake. . . . Some years electric light lines were run out to Smelt Town [on the lake] and each night the town on the lake would be all aglow with hundreds of lights."

Case

Collecting sap for that fabulous Benzie County maple syrup

"Mrs. S. went to a sugar party today"

"Uncle Charlie had a sugar bush . . .THE REAL THING. The bush was in a stand of virgin maples and for a few weeks in early spring each year it was just about the sweetest spot in all creation.

Promptly after school, each day a group of fortunate boys and girls would appear at the sugar bush to gather the day's run of sap. They had no thought or desire for financial remuneration for the rewards for these chores were beyond price.

Set a little aside from the principal boiling pans was a smaller pan which attracted the most attention from the young helpers after the sap was all gathered. In it was bubbling an ever thickening concoction being readied for that incomparable delicacy known as maple wax. When it was just right, it would be spread over clean snow in a large wash tub and then hardening but still warm would be scooped up with hand made wooden paddles and eaten by the impatiently waiting children. This was the 'sugaring off.' Years and dulled taste buds can never fade the memory of the taste of those gobs of wax to those whose mouths still water at the thought."

Case

The smelt run at Cold Creek ~ Beulah

Annual Smelt Run ~ Beulah ~ Spring c.1931

"The peak year of the Beulah Smelt Runs was 1927...that was the year the Governor [Green] came to town. . . .His excellency was an avid sportsman and loved fishing, . . . on Wednesday morning he determined to sling the cares of office aside and go up to Beulah where he could join thousands of his constituents in floundering around in Cold Creek with a short handled net, an instrument so necessary in catching the smelt and so convenient to trip or jab a too close fellow fisherman. . . ."

"A Pathe News cameraman was on hand to film the Governor's plunge into the creek. Car horns honked, lights flashed, men shouted, women screamed, boys whistled, girls squealed, and dogs barked. . . . No one remembers if anyone knew how many smelt the Governor netted that evening but the occasion itself is remembered and known by all its survivors as the grandest of all nights of the Beulah Smelt Runs."

Case

Benzonia's Baseball Team ~ 1913

1950s Old Timers' Team

Frankfort had a baseball team in the 1880s. In the 1920s, the managers began re-cruiting players and scheduling some of the best competitions in the Midwest. From 1953-1956, it hosted the National Baseball Congress State Tournaments. In 1954 this team became the smallest city team in Michigan history to win the NBC tournament title. The team folded in 1967.

Sandman

Showing off their new bicycles ~ c.1900

Bicycles - a harbinger of spring!

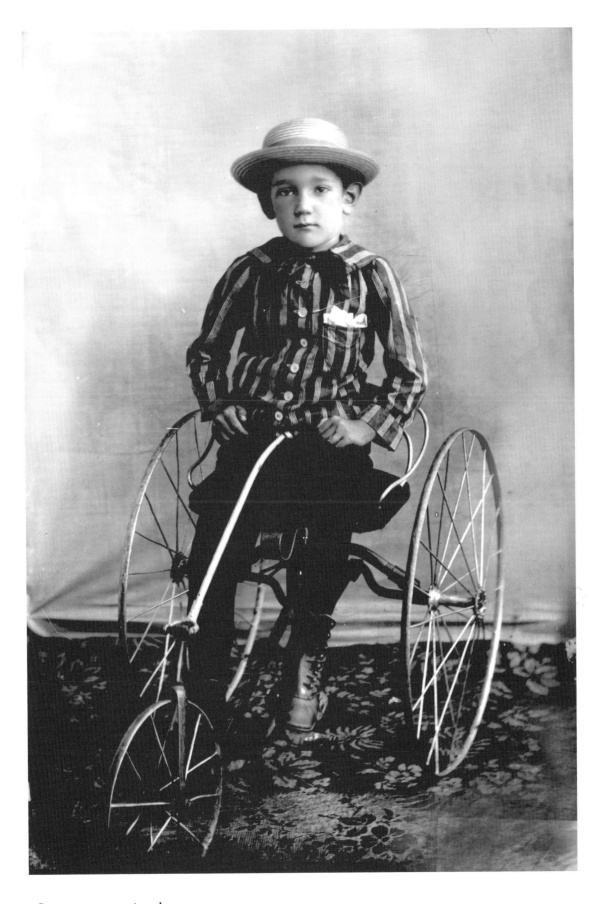

Love my new tricycle

Championship golfing came to Benzie County ~ Crystal Downs Club House ~ 1936

On the green at Crystal Downs

In 1926, property was purchased for the Crystal Downs Country Club. Improvements included a nine hole golf course - the first in the Benzie County area. The fee to play golf was 75 cents.

Wow ~ what a catch! ~ plenty of fish and plenty of folks to eat them

Fishing at its best ~ showing off the great fishing at Robinson's Resort ~ Crystal Lake ~ 1900

"Triplets" ~ 1915

"Ladies" enjoy fishing too ~ Crystal Lake

Nothing tastes better than freshly caught fish cooked over the open campfire ~ c.1920

Fishing was great ~ that fishing hole will never be the same!

Some of life's pleasures never change ~ the future is in good hands

"On nearing the stream, I picked up the pleasant rippling sound of water flowing over rocks and swirling around half submerged logs. A thin, supple maple sapling was cut and trimmed, the fishline tied on, hook added, and a small split-shot clamped on with my teeth. All the good fishing holes were familiar to me so I crept up to a large, rotting log that angled past way across the stream. I threaded a worm on the hook and tossed out a few feet upstream of the log. As the current pulled the bait toward a dark recess cut under the log, a brightly colored object darted out, sucked on the worm, and shot back for its lair. I instantly set the hook before the fish could swallow the bait. The tip of the little maple danced an Irish jig, telling me I had my first trout of the day."

Barnard

221

Benzie County's hard working families took time to play along the way and enjoy the beauty of their surroundings ~ tourists also joined in the fun

The Lake Michigan "Two Step"

We're here!!

Nothing like cooling off at the old swimming hole on a hot summer day

"Upstream a few yards was the crown jewel of swimming holes; deep, dark water, out of the main current, under a large overhanging tree. Obviously, this hole was meant for good swimmers, of which I wasn't yet a member. The remedy came one day in the blink-of-an-eye; one of the older boys pushed me in. He knew how to swim so I wasn't in much danger, but I wasn't about to depend on that. The old adage 'sink or swim' took over. I swam."

Barnard

Oh! It's colder than we thought ~ challenging Lake Michigan's powerful surf

You go first ~ Crystal Lake

"I have swam in many places over the years; lakes, swimming pools, even in a couple of other countries. And who could ask for anything better than the white sand and azure waters of Crystal Lake."

Barnard

Ladies-in-wading

Waiting for a ride on the "Sunny Side" ~ Lake Ann ~ c.1914

A lovely day for a family outing ~ wheels were used to take the boat ashore, and to prevent the passengers from getting wet

The "Oberlin"   *Aquaplane ~ tricky fun! ~ c.1950*

Before the start of the race ~ Crystal Lake Yacht Club ~ 1949

"The Crystal Lake Boat Club had a membership of over ninety men. The club was founded soon after the turn of the century. The membership was comprised of local and summer residents. A number of the members owned power boats that competed in races, generally on Saturdays during the summer. These races were held at the Beulah end of the lake. Families from all over the area came to watch the races. The last race of the season was for the 'Ladies Challenge Cup' - a sterling silver cup with the name of each winner engraved on the side of the cup. The first race was in 1909 and the last was in 1915. The last boat to win in 1915 was the 'Oberlin' owned by Robert Kirshner, whose family had summered on Crystal Lake since 1902."

Kirshner

A Barn Stormer's flying boat on the Crystal Lake beach ~ Beulah ~ 1913

What a delightful day ~ we rented a boat and floated down Platte River

Return trip was easy ~ tied together we were pulled back up the Platte River ~ c.1948

Glider soaring above Elberta Beach

"About 1932 the first Soaring Meet was held on the Elberta Municipal Beach. The meet was promoted by Frankfort interests and it was determined by the experts involved that the Elberta Lake Michigan Beach was one of the most suitable places for launching, landing, and bluff soaring with gliders, especially with a west wind."

Blacklock

Taking off from the airport connected to a tow line ~ late 1930s

"Throughout the history of Frankfort, 'nothing has dominated a period of time more than the sport of gliding during the late 1930s.' The entire town was involved. The gliding school was the first community backed in the nation and the sailplane factory was one of the largest in the United States. The winds off Lake Michigan gave the town more soaring days per year than any other site. . . . When a Frankfort businessman was late for dinner, his wife only shrugged and said, 'Must be a good soaring day.' The truant officers had learned to make a daily scrutiny of the glider field."

Bixby & Sandman

233

Spotted Tails Camp ~ Honor ~ November 22, 1900

Hunting and fishing just seem to go together. For many folks this was more than a sport. They counted on their bounty for the dinner table. Hunting clubs were very popular.

A successful day of hunting rabbits with the hounds

The Elberta Rod and Gun Club "was organized in the 1930s for the purpose of fellowship among the sportsmen of Elberta and to further the hunting and fishing in the area. Many Chinese Pheasants were hatched and raised by the members and released on the hills of the village and the surrounding area."

The Benzie Sportsman's Club "was organized in Elberta in the 1940s, more or less a revival of the old gun club. The area was expanded to cover anyone who might be interested to join. The club was pretty well local for a while then started meeting in various communities of Benzie County."

Blacklock

The "Hermit of Platte Lake" at his hunting camp ~ 1903

*In our youth we learned to fish
and hunt*

"The son of a Point Betsie keeper walked along the beach to school carrying a five shot repeater colt rifle and a gunny sack. On his way home he was supposed to shoot game, put it in the gunny sack, and bring it home for dinner. No game—no dinner."

Pearson

Life's Little Pleasures

They made me stand still!

Sitting Pretty ~ 1897

"The 'Life's Little Pleasures' photographs have captured the moment, that instant in time that cannot be repeated. The photographs allow one to visualize the days of yore, to spark a memory, and to get lost in reverie."

Laarman

Big brother in charge ~ what do I do now?

The simple pleasures of childhood

"Over we go!"

The "push me, pull you" gang

"That little wagon has given countless hours of pleasure to three generations of children-and not a few adults. It has hauled cords of stove wood, garden produce, groceries, reluctant cats and dogs and manure. Our parents bought it for my brothers and me. How they ever came up with the three or four dollars to purchase it is beyond me. Our presents were almost always homemade so this was something very special."

Barnard

Impatiently waiting for a ride when the work was done

Taking a family portrait was a very serious matter ~ William Saga and family
~ Honor c.1910

Several generations of the Wolfe Family ~ Glen Rhoda ~ c.1906

"Health and happiness seemed to come from hard work when we had to hike through the woods and along the beach for provender. Gingersnaps, bean soup, potato soup, tomato soup, oatmeal, salt pork, dried beef with the fish we caught and berries we picked were our menus. It was a great change when a road built at the foot of the bluff brought milk, butter, eggs and vegetables right to our pump steps."

Cornelia Weitzel Wolfe (1864-1939)

Bringing the "fixings" for a corn roast on the beach

Enjoying warmth and fellowship around a glowing fire

"In the early days: "There were 'gatherings' of young people in a merry group around the bonfires of huge log heaps in the soft summer evenings and amid the wild surroundings was enacted many a drama that blossomed into a life time of mutual happiness. There was a friendliness and warmth in those good old days."

Case

Early aerobics ~ Benzonia Academy

Two sides to those "sophisticated ladies"

Bathing Beauties chorus line ~ 1915

Hmmm ~ what are they up to?

Congregational Summer Assembly Dining Hall ~ Assembly bus waiting to take passengers into town

"By the early 1920s, there were several Crystal Lake Resorts which were enjoyed by many. The Congregational Summer Assembly and the Christian (Disciples of Christ) Assembly became areas of permanent summer homes for many families from surrounding states. Both organizations are still very active in the summer months."

Bixby & Sandman

"The Congregational Summer Assembly has attracted to it each summer many persons of eminence in Congregational circles who have shared in its activities and contributed to its effectiveness as a summer resort with a religious background and heritage."

Sunday stroll after church at Bennett Auditorium ~ Congregational Summer Assembly ~ 1916

Gathering for a dinner party at a CSA tent ~ 1907

A "Special Day was known as the Congregational Summer Assembly - Benzonia Church Day. There would be an out-of-doors worship service in the forenoon, followed by a picnic dinner and in the afternoon an inspirational program featuring special music and short talks by representatives of the participating groups. They were memorable and happy occasions."

Case

Gathering for the Fourth of July celebration ~ Beulah

"The times I liked best going to grandmother's house were on July 4th. For years on that day the whole clan would gather, bringing tons of delicious food, dozens of kids overrunning the place, and grownups shooting their deer rifles into the gravel pit, pitching horseshoes, and telling old-time stories. Usually some young buck, out to prove himself, got a wrestling match going. Grandfather took a back seat to no one."

Barnard

Sunflower Express ~ Thompsonville Fair ~ 1917

Clowning around

After the parade, "the mounds of food were something to behold. There may not have been any money in those Depression times, but country people grew and canned their own food. Homemade ice cream, pies, cakes, potato salad, and on and on. It was almost enough to make a kid willing to wash behind his ears and slip into his Sunday knickers."

Barnard

Everyone wanted to play in this early Honor Band ~ some even wore their uniforms

Strike up the band ~ South Frankfort Band on steps of John Baver building ~ 1896

Even the early origins of a band were thought to be newsworthy:
"Bendon soon expects to have a band, some of the instruments are already here."

Benzie Banner
March 27, 1913

254

Music has always been important in Benzie County ~ an all-girl band ~ Frankfort

Thompsonville City Band ~ all dressed up and ready to perform

"Camp Ohio" ~ early family camp on Lake Michigan Bluffs ~ August 1, 1910

Benzie County became well known as the perfect campground that allowed everyone to enjoy nature at its finest.

Sunday Service at Camp Roy

All on board and ready to go!

"Red's Gang was a day camp for young boys in the 1930s. Each day they were picked up at 9:00 a.m. for a fun-filled day of swimming, softball and camping but always with a focus on character building. They often competed with other camps in the area."

Beidler

Off for an overnight camping trip with their bed rolls ~ Camp Lookout ~ a summer camp for boys ~ c.1940s

Waiting to start a day filled with adventure ~ Camp Lookout ~ c.1940s

Free to be me

"There was nothing better than, on a boiling hot July day, going . . . Swimming, . . . and the neatest way to go in was buck naked. You felt free as an otter, but there were hazards involved. Such as the day our lady teacher brought some of the girls around for an outing."

Barnard

Butterfly Brigade ~ Camp Lookout ~ c.1940s

Sailing, one of the skills learned at Crystalaire Camp for girls

Everybody learned to canoe!

Look at that form ! ~ Crystalaire Camp ~ c.1930s

Whitecaps in Crystal Lake ~ remember those?

And the delightful camp experience ends with a ride, beautiful sunset, and many memories

"It has been said by learned scholars that one should not dwell in the past. I'll go along with that premise, but I see nothing wrong with deriving pleasure in remembering those 'Good Old Days.' Perhaps we gloss over the hard times, remembering only that which gives us gratification. That also is as it should be."

Barnard

Reflections

"The Greatest of Days"

"Which day of your life is the greatest of days?
The shadows of years hover over the head
of the man that I questioned:
"I would yield my best praise
to a yesterday vanished and buried,"
he said.

"As the greatest of days which would you make
your choice?"
I asked of a man in the flush of his prime.
"Why today is the season in which I rejoice;
Tis the zenith, the apex, the pivotal time."

To a youth I next turned; "Which is your greatest
day?"
The sunrise of hopefulness beamed from his eyes;
In a thrice a whole lifetime he seemed to survey—
"Why tomorrow's the day I singly prize."

Howard

"Sooner or later you must move down an unknown road that leads
beyond the range of the imagination . . . .

Life becomes exciting
just because it is life."

Catton (1899-1978)

Bibliography

Anderson, Charles. <u>Memo's of Betsie Bay A History of Frankfort.</u>

Barnard, Don. <u>Growing Up Stories.</u> 1996.

Bixby, Florence, and Pete Sandman. <u>Port City Prospectives.</u> Frankfort: BaySide Printing, Inc., 2000.

Blacklock, Allen B. <u>Blacklock's History of Elberta.</u> 1975

Brosier, Emily Travis. <u>Lake Ann – Small But Friendly.</u> Frankfort: BaySide Printing, Inc., 1997.

Case, Leonard. <u>Benzie County A Bicentennial Reader.</u> Benzonia: Benzie County Bi-Centennial Commission, 1976.

Case, Leonard L. <u>The Crystal Gazer.</u> Manistee: J. B. Publications, 1985.

Catton, Bruce. <u>Waiting for the Morning Train.</u> Garden City: Doubleday & Company, Inc., 1972.

Frederickson, Arthur C. and Lucy F. <u>Frederickson's History of the Ann Arbor Auto and Train Ferries.</u> Benton Harbor: Patterson Printing, 1994.

Gibbs, Bryce. <u>Thompsonville A History.</u> 1976.

Howard, John H. <u>Mint O' The Muse.</u> Boston: The Christopher Publishing House, 1929.

Howard, John H. <u>The Story of Frankfort.</u> City Council of Frankfort, Michigan, 1930.

Overlease, William and Edith. <u>Daylight in the Swamp.</u> Frankfort: BaySide Printing, Inc. 1996.

Saunders, J. W. and George R. Robinson. <u>Benzie County, Michigan Summerland of Recreation and Rest.</u> Benzie County Information Bureau, 1916.

Seabury, Charles Ward. <u>The History and Growth of Frankfort, Michigan.</u>

Stadtfeld, Curtis K. <u>From the Land and Back.</u> New York: Charles Scribner's Sons, 1972.

Stocking, Kathleen. <u>Lake Country.</u> Ann Arbor: The University of Michigan Press, 1994.

(U. S.) War Department Commission on Training Camp Activities. <u>U. S. Army Song Book.</u> Washington, 1918.

Walling, H. F., C. E. <u>1873 Atlas of the State of Michigan.</u> Detroit: R. M. & S. T. Tackabury, 1873.

Weeks, George. <u>Mem-ka-weh.</u> Traverse City: Grand Traverse Band of Ottawa and Chippewa Indians Village Press, Inc, 1992.

<u>The Traverse Region</u> Chicago: H. R. Page & Co., 1884.

Credits & Information

This section contains the names of donors of the photographs. It also lists additional information, such as places, identification of photographic subjects, where known, dates, etc. The Benzie Area Historical Society is only listing information that is in its collection, or has been passed on by notations on the photographs received by donors, etc.. The Society asks that you contact the Benzie Area Historical Museum if you have corrections, additions, or identifications related to the photographs, or the content of this book.

Page   Source of Photographs & Information

Cover *Watervale*
II   *Benzie Area Historical Society*
       Back Row: Left to Right: Miss Winifred Waters (Teacher); Leslie Smith; (?); Bertha Ellis
       Front Row: Left to Right: Etta Gilbert; John Ehman; Iza Smith
2   *Benzie Area Historical Society*
3   *History of Images of Benzie County, MI*, Old Indian Trail
4   *Collier collection*
7   *Benzie Shores District Library* "Roy Oliver remembers seeing those two schooners on the beach just north of the Frankfort pier in the fall of 1894." *Charles W. Seabury* (photo given to Seabury by Roy Oliver).
8   *Benzie Area Historical Society*
9   *Benzie Area Historical Society: Fred Water's Glass Plates*
10   *Benzie Area Historical Society: C. Anderson collection*
12   *Benzie Area Historical Society:* Benzonia Township
13   *Holmes collection*
14   *Benzie Area Historical Society*
15   *Sandman collection*
16   *Benzie Area Historical Society*
17   *Harrison collection*
18   *Benzie Area Historical Society* ~ near Empire or Case's Pond
19   *Benzie Shores District Library* ~ log drive on the Betsie River
20   *Benzie Area Historical Society*
21a   *Anderson collection* ~ "B…. Wilson lifting logs with steam driven machine on railroad tracks."
21b   *Empire Museum*
22   *Benzie Area Historical Society:* ~ Platte Edgewater Mill ~ owned and operated by Little Bros.
23   *Slater collection* ~ c.1910
24a   *Bailey collection*
24b   *Forrester collection*
25   *Benzie Area Historical Society: Frederickson collection*
26   *Benzie Area Historical Society: Fred Water's Glass Plates*
27   *Slater collection*
28   *Slater collection*
29   *Slater collection*
30a   *Benzie Area Historical Society: Eldridge collection*
30b   *Olsen collection*
31   *Slater collection*
32   *Benzie Area Historical Society: Weaver collection* ~ Mrs. Joe Covey ~ Honor
33   *Benzie Area Historical Society: Weaver collection* ~ John Twiddle Farm, south of Empire on the Benzie-Leelanau County Line; driver of oxen: Owen Sherwood (photo taken by Ray Edwards)

Page   Source of Photographs & Information

163   *Benzie Area Historical Society ~* In front of: Midway Saloon; Smith Barber Shop; Mrs. Dundon's Bakery & Restaurant Note village sprinkler for watering streets.
Two men on Right: Ed & Raleigh Ward; man with apron on Left: John Rossidor (bartender); Man in white overalls: John Schaeffer

164   *Benzie Area Historical Society ~ Sharp Ridout collection ~* Leslie W. Northrup

165   *White collection*

166a   *Olsen collection*

166b   *Benzie Area Historical Society*

167a   *Benzie Area Historical Society ~ Sharp Ridout collection ~* Will Lovett; John Sherman; Byron Doty; Clarence Moody; Tony Monroe; Mr. Van Dam; Mr. J. Blanchard

167b   *Harrison collection*

168   *Benzie Area Historical Society ~* Lewis Carey; Mr. Hallack

169   *Harrison collection ~ Lake Street*

170   *Benzie Area Historical Society*

171a   *Benzie Area Historical Society ~ Frederickson collection ~* Frankfort's first telephone office (in George R. Robinson's office ~ corner of Fifth and Main) ~ Rose E. Fine, first operator

171b   *Benzie Area Historical Society*

172   *Benzie Area Historical Society ~ Banktson collection*

173a   *Benzie Area Historical Society ~ Eldridge collection*

173b   *Sandman collection*

174a   *Sandman collection*

174b   *Beidler collection*

177   *Benzie Area Historical Society*

178   *Benzie Area Historical Society*

179a   *Benzie Area Historical Society*

179b   *Benzie Area Historical Society*

180   *Benzie Area Historical Society*

181   *Benzie Area Historical Society ~* Althea Petritz in striped dress

182   *Benzie Area Historical Society*

183   *Beidler collection ~* Mrs. Doyle; Mrs. Hofstetter; Edith Classens; Anna Collier; Mrs. Penfold; Mrs. Fairchild

184a   *Benzie Area Historical Society ~* Person far left: Hiram Stanley; Far Right: Charles Raymond

184b   *Benzie Area Historical Society*

185   *Benzie Area Historical Society ~* Alfred ____; Tom Johnson ~ first Frankfort volunteers WWI

186a   *Bailey collection ~* Alex Wayashe

186b   *Benzie Area Historical Society ~* Robert Catton; Bruce Catton

187   *Benzie Area Historical Society ~* Madonna Nolan Cussans; Agnes Nolan Barnett

188   *Benzie Area Historical Society ~* Second Row, Seventh from Right: Lt. (SG) W. Robert Catton, Chaplain

190   *Benzie Area Historical Society*

191   *Benzie Area Historical Society ~* Frankfort teachers: Right: Emma Johanna Maria Nelson (Mrs. Ole E. Olsen)

192   *White collection*

193   *Anderson collection*

194   *Beidler collection*

195   *Anderson collection*

196   *Benzie Area Historical Society*

197a   *Kirshner collection*

197b   *Benzie Area Historical Society*

198   *Harrison collection*

Page   Source of Photographs & Information

Page   Source of Photographs & Information